Et Voilà!

A Simple French Baking Love Story

Et Voilà!

A Simple French Baking Love Story

MANON LAGRÈVE

OH EDITIONS

Photography by Nassima Rothacker

Contents

Introduction

In France, the term *pâtisser*, 'to bake', is mostly used when talking about a professional *pâtissier*, not a home baker. Instead, we simply *faire un gâteau*, 'make a cake', for a weekly dessert or a Sunday family meal – a simple sweet treat, made without fuss, for the joy of sharing.

This is what this book is about – French classics, simplified or with a twist. All of these recipes can be made in the comfort of your home, using a basic springform tin or the standard baking tray that is probably already lurking in a kitchen drawer. Baking is my love language. I believe you don't need to train as a baker to be able to bake. I want people to know that a cake with a fancy French name does not have to be difficult or pretentious to make. My *maman* (mum) and my grandmas ran a farm, so they didn't have the time to spend hours baking, but even so there was always a homemade dessert at every meal.

Let me take you back a little bit into my childhood, to where my love for food, and particularly desserts and sweet things, started ...

I was born in a small village in rural Brittany in December 1991. The second of three children who grew up at Maman and Papa's farm, napping in cardboard boxes softened by a cushion. Maman took over and developed her parents' egg farm, and with my father created their own brand, Les Oeufs Coquelin. It is safe to say we never ran out of eggs at home, which definitely contributed to my love of cakes! But more than that, we were surrounded by incredible locally farmed products, home-grown fruits, vegetables and our own cattle.

Almost every month at my grandparents' all our aunties, uncles and cousins joined together for a family meal and would bring something they had farmed or prepared. On Papa's side, my grandma, Mamie Suzanne, and my late grandpa, Papi Pierre, made the most delicious feasts. From a rabbit stew to roast beef, with *frites* made with home-grown potatoes and haricot beans from the garden. *Tonton* (Uncle) Alain would bring lots of whole milk from his farm, and *Tonton* Jean Pierre some charcuterie from his butcher's shop. We'd take crates of eggs for everyone, and we'd all swap our homemade jams.

And it was exactly the same on Maman's side. *Tonton* Jean Bernard from Bordeaux has been making the most delicious wine for decades, wines that are available at *Tonton* Jean Charles' restaurant, Le Bretagne. Mamie Gilberte raises pigeons and lambs, grows tonnes of fruits and makes kilos of jams!

There was never a feast without at least one dessert. Our lunches (which always turned into dinner, after a short walk around the countryside) lasted for hours, leaving us children waiting impatiently for what we wanted the most: *le dessert*! Because in most French homes, there is ALWAYS dessert, and I still have a dessert every single night. The most frequent desserts were simple, like the ones you can find in Chapter 1 – *Clafoutis aux Fruits de Saisons* (Seasonal Fruit Clafoutis, p. 41), *Mousse au Chocolat de Maman* (Maman's Chocolate Mousse, p. 42) or *Tiramisu aux Fraises D'été* (Summer Strawberry Tiramisu, p. 29). On special occasions, Mamie Suzanne would buy some *pâtisseries* from the local *boulangerie*. I have shared my simplified versions of our family favourites in Chapter 3 – the *Paris Brest* (Paris Brest, p. 106) or *Éclair au Chocolat Praliné* (Chocolate Praliné Éclair, p. 101).

Maman was, and still is in my eyes, the most impressive cook. I know of the hours and hours she has spent in the kitchen, making sure her children always had delicious meals and homemade afternoon treats (Chapter 4), or that her friends coming at the weekend had a variety of appetisers, starter, main, cheese platter and dessert with cream or some other extra. Papa always guided us as we set the table and helped Maman, while he chose and opened the wine. Our house was always full, and it always will be, as I return to Brittany often with my daughter, Fleur, so she can capture its essence too.

For me, all of these moments preparing food, sharing food, talking about food, arguing about food, is simply love. I am grateful to have been raised in a family where, even if the words 'I love you' were not often said, I always knew how much *amour* there was surrounding us.

I hope you will enjoy making and sharing my recipes with people you love, because really there is no better feeling than having a bit of *la belle vie* (the good life).

BEFORE YOU START

A Note on the Ingredients

The majority of the ingredients for my recipes are easily obtainable in all supermarkets. I always shop seasonally, so you will be able to make all of my recipes in spring and summer, and maybe swap to a chocolate or caramel one in the winter. Alternatively, buying good-quality frozen or canned fruits is better than buying off-season fruit, which come from very far away or might be tasteless.

For the rest of the ingredients, I always try to buy the best local produce. There are two specific products that you may need to get online – praliné paste (that you can also make yourself, p. 106) and tonka beans (which are also a great, cheaper alternative to vanilla bean paste).

Equipment

I believe that having a few key baking utensils in your kitchen will make it much more enjoyable and easier for you to make and bake desserts. Over the years, I have cooked in many unequipped kitchens, but thanks to experience and confidence, I can pretty much whip up anything wherever I am, and I know you can too!

It is definitely a time-saver to own a stand-alone mixer or have a few piping bags to hand. I guess that also makes me think of my mamies, who without the luxury of a thermostat oven or an electric mixer still baked delicious goods. My Mamie Suzanne even made her own butter, either using it or selling it at the *marché* at the weekend to make a bit of extra money for the family. She used a wooden *baratte*, or churn (which we still have), to separate the fat from the water in the milk and make butter. It took over an hour of hard work just to make 500g (1lb 2oz) of butter. So thank you modern life for bringing us ready-made butter and electric power!

I have pretty much classified these items by order of importance, and you will hopefully already have the first five items, which means you will be able to make at least half of the recipes in the book!

BAKING TINS

Two 23cm (9in) springform round tins; a 31cm (12in) rectangular baking tin; a fluted 23cm (9in) tart tin; ramekins; individual tins for madeleines.

Starting with the basics, you will need a tin in which to bake your cake or clafoutis. All the cake recipes are adapted to a standard 23cm (9in) round tin, which also works with a rectangular tin or a loaf tin. There are of course plenty of other shaped tins, such as Bundt tins. You can also make all of the cake recipes as tiered cakes, using two 15cm (6in) round cake tins.

LARGE MIXING BOWL

The majority of my recipes are achievable using just a bowl and the rest of first five utensils in this list. It also means you can make them on holidays, in your student home, at your best friend's house – anywhere that has an oven.

THERMOSTAT OVEN

I know that ovens vary in power, especially if they are old. All the oven temperatures given in these recipes are for an electric fan oven. If you do not have a fan-assisted oven, increase the temperature by 20°C (about 50°F). An oven thermometer is an excellent and affordable tool, which will allow you to know the true temperature of your oven. I encourage you to have a look at the 'Is it cooked?' feature overleaf to help you to figure out your oven and understand it better. There are, of course, a few no-bake recipes, like the *Mousse au Chocolat de Maman* (Maman's Chocolate Mousse, p. 42) or the *Guimauves Enrobé de Chocolat* (Chocolate-covered Marshmallows, p. 165).

ELECTRIC SCALE

Trust me, 10g more or less of anything in all of these recipes will NOT mess up your bake, but I still encourage you to get a precise electric scale as it is much easier! I have included cup measurements if you prefer to use them, but I do think that using a scale leads to less baking fails as they give a much more accurate measurement. I also find it much more satisfying and handier to have all of my ingredients measured in little bowls before I start cooking – it allows you to easily follow the recipe and not miss any steps or ingredients.

SPATULA AND WHISK

It always makes baking easier if you have these two items in your kitchen. A whisk is useful for whipping up a Chantilly cream, or whisking any cake batter. The spatula will help you to fold in whipped egg whites, scrape the side of the bowl and even smooth a buttercream or cake batter before baking.

CERAMIC BLIND-BAKING BALLS

Essential if you re making your own pastries. Ceramic ones are pretty cheap to buy but if you don't have any, dried peas, rice, beans or any other pulses will do the trick.

PASTRY BRUSH

If you are planning on making any *pâtisserie*, I find a pastry brush very handy. It can even be a paintbrush, as long as it has soft and food-safe bristles. Whether it is to brush off the flour in between your croissant layers or to brush some egg wash on top of your choux pastries to make them golden, you will find it useful!

LARGE BAKING TRAY AND REUSABLE SILICON MAT

If you are planning to make some biscuits or *pâtisserie*, these are essential. I like to use reusable silicon mats, as I often make cookies, croissants and choux at home.

ELECTRIC MIXER WITH A WHISK AND HOOK ATTACHMENT

It was always my dream to have my own electric stand mixer, and it is still one of my favourite items in my kitchen to date. It is essential when it comes to making meringues, buttercream or kneading doughs for *viennoiseries*. As I mentioned, not having one doesn't mean you won't be able to bake most of the recipes in this book, but I would recommend purchasing a cheaper hand-held electric mixer to figure out how often you use it. You will quickly know whether you are ready for the bigger one.

PIPING BAGS (PROFESSIONAL)

Piping bags can be so useful! You don't have to know how to 'pipe' to use these, they can be used to make choux, to fill up your chocolate mousse ramekins, or to spread madeleine batter or buttercream on a cake.

1CM (½IN) ROUND/STAR-SHAPED NOZZLE

Another important item that will help you make your *pâtisserie*! There is also nothing more satisfying than piping some Chantilly cream on top of a choux or filling an éclair with *crème pâtissière*. I like to use large nozzles, and you only need a couple!

Troubleshooting, Hacks and Finishing Touches

PREPARING THE TIN

Always grease or line your tin so you can easily remove your dessert to serve. My foolproof lining method is:

1. Generously butter the tin. Use a pastry brush and some softened butter at room temperature. It is important not to melt it, otherwise the butter won't stick to the sides of your tins.

2. Add one tablespoon of plain (all-purpose) flour to the tin and just shake it around so the flour coats all of the tin. Tap the side of the tin to remove excess flour. This will create a layer that will stop your cake sticking when baked. I use the same technique for Bundt cakes and any special tins, like Madeleine trays.

3. Finally, if your cake tin is a bit rusty (we all have them), you can put a piece of baking paper at the bottom of the tin, on top of the butter, so it sticks. You can then sprinkle the flour on the sides.

IS IT COOKED?

All temperatures and timings in this book are for fan ovens. But ovens differ, so you might have to adjust the baking time. Don't worry, I have got you.

1. For cakes and sponges, the easiest way to check if it is baked through is to insert a skewer (or a small sharp knife) into the middle of your cake. If it comes out completely clean, it is cooked. If it comes out with some batter stuck to it, put it back in the oven and bake for an extra 5 minutes at a time until cooked.

2. For brioches and bread, you can quickly knock the bottom of the tin – if it makes a hollow sound, it is cooked; if it makes a deep sound, put it back in the oven for an extra 5 minutes at a time.

3. For any pastry, you want it to be a deep golden colour.

MY CAKE IS STUCK TO THE TIN, WHAT DO I DO?

This will hopefully be avoided if you follow my recommendations on greasing and lining, but if it still won't budge, here are a few tips:

1. Never wait more than 5 minutes to unmould your cakes. The longer you wait, the more the sugar sets and caramelises around the cake, making it harder to remove from its tin.

2. Use a sharp knife around the sides of the cake to create a little gap.

3. Turn the tin and cake upside down onto a plate, and use the knife to scrape and help the bottom of the tin to unstick.

4. It will come out eventually, and if you have still some cake stuck at the bottom of the tin, just carefully remove with a knife and place it where it belongs.

5. You can now turn the cake right way up and no one will ever know it got stuck. Alternatively cover it with some *Glaçage au Mascarpone* (Mascarpone Icing/Frosting, p. 178) or *Ganache Montée* (Whipped Ganache, p. 178).

HOW DO I MAKE IT LOOK PRETTY?

My speciality is making something simple look more impressive. I always have at home:

1. Fresh flowers: they can be edible, but it's not necessary as long as they have not been sprayed with pesticides and you remove them before slicing. The addition of a flower on top of a cake, or a few petals here and there, can make all the difference.

2. Freshly cut fruits: depending on the recipe, additionally placing some of its key fresh ingredients on top is always a good idea.

3. Something powdery to dust the top (great for a burnt cake): icing (confectioners') sugar, cocoa powder or freeze-dried raspberries.

4. Something nutty: crushed pistachios, slivered almonds, roasted hazelnuts or desiccated (dried shredded) coconut.

5. A ganache, some icing, or even some jam, for topping.

MY CAKE HAS RISEN ON TOP, HOW DO I STACK IT?

If you want to make a tiered cake (all the recipes in Chapter 2, for instance, can make two 15cm/6in sponges), the most important thing to do is cut the top of the cake flat. Use a serrated knife and start by tracing an even line on the sides of the top of the cake you want to cut, then gradually cut deeper and deeper to get a flat and even top.

HOW TO MELT CHOCOLATE

1. *Au bain marie*: put the chocolate into a heatproof bowl and place on top of a pan filled with water, ensuring the water is not touching the base of the bowl. Heat the pan over a medium heat for 3–5 minutes or until the chocolate starts to melt evenly, stirring occasionally.

2. In the microwave: place the chocolate into a microwave-safe dish and microwave on full power for 30 seconds at a time. Repeat as necessary, stirring in between to evenly melt the chocolate.

If I have to melt some butter with chocolate, or some milk and chocolate, I just put everything straight into a pan and heat over a medium heat. It will take 3–5 minutes for the chocolate to melt.

HOW TO BRING BUTTER TO ROOM TEMPERATURE

Often a recipe will say 'butter at room temperature', which needs the butter to be out of the fridge 3 hours beforehand. If you are like me and don't always plan to bake, here's my trick. When my oven is preheating, I dice the butter, put it in an ovenproof dish, then leave it in the base of the oven for a few minutes until it is soft and ready to use.

EN DESSERT

Desserts

This chapter is about everyday desserts. For my family and friends – I could even generalise and say the majority of French households – every meal is three courses, which means we always finish with something sweet, whether it is a *tartine* with jam and butter, a yoghurt or a simple homemade dessert like those in this chapter. All the recipes in this section are quick, unapologetically simple and modest, but I'll show you how to make them shine with a few tricks.

Most of these desserts can be made the day before, so they are perfect for dinner parties when you don't want to stress with cooking once your guests have arrived or after a couple of glasses of wine! Some recipes are easily adaptable depending on the season and when fruits are available, with some traditional family recipes from my Mamie Suzanne and my maman thrown in for good measure.

TARTES FINES AUX FIGUES ET À LA FRANGIPANE

Fig and Almond Frangipane Tarts

There were not many things that my maman would buy ready-made, but puff pastry was one such ingredient. I don't blame anyone who does this, especially with the great quality ones at most supermarkets. Figs were picked in my auntie's garden in Bordeaux in the summer, and a lot of *tartes fines* or *confiture de figues* were made with them. A ripe fig is my ultimate fruit, and you can find several varieties in your local grocers. The frangipane adds some richness and nuttiness to complement the subtle fig taste.

Makes: 4 tarts

Special equipment:

a baking sheet, four 12cm (4½in) round tartlet tins

Ingredients:

1 sheet of puff pastry
plain (all-purpose) flour, for dusting
75g (3oz) salted butter, at room temperature
100g (3½oz/scant ½ cup) caster (superfine) sugar
1 large egg, plus 1 egg yolk for brushing
150g (5oz/1½ cups) ground almonds
8 figs
3 tbsp honey

Tip: You can drizzle some extra honey on top to make the tart filling look shiny, and serve these warm with vanilla ice cream.

1. Preheat the oven to 180°C fan (400°F/gas 6).

2. Roll out the pastry on a work surface that's lightly dusted with flour. Cut out four circles of pastry, each 12cm (4½in) in diameter, and place on the baking sheet, evenly spaced. Cut four long strips from the remaining pastry, and place one around the outer circle of each little tart as a raised rim, sealing it to the pastry beneath with a little water. Use a fork to prick little holes on the base of each tart, then place in the fridge while you make the frangipane.

3. Using a spatula, cream the butter with the sugar in a bowl until it is light and fluffy. Stir in the egg and finally the ground almonds. It should form a paste that is easy to spread. Spread 2 tablespoons of this frangipane on top of each of the chilled pastry cases, using a spoon to even it out.

4. Slice the figs thinly and gently place on top of the frangipane. Drizzle some honey over the figs and use a pastry brush to brush some egg yolk over the uncovered pastry edges.

5. Bake in the oven for 20 minutes until the pastry is cooked and golden.

FAR BRETON

Prune Flan

This is one of those desserts that takes five minutes to make and that you can then forget about while it's in the oven. You will find *far Breton* everywhere in Brittany – a non-expensive, simple, flan-like cake with prunes to sweeten it up. Maman makes a ton of them when she knows she has some people coming over to the farm or when she needs to make a quick dessert for lunch. Moreish is the word I would use for my *far Breton* as it is very hard to leave one piece uneaten on the tray!

Serves: 6 generously

Special equipment:

30cm (12in) traybake tin or 30cm (12in) round tin

Ingredients:

5 eggs
100g (3½oz/scant ½ cup) caster (superfine) sugar
500ml (18fl oz/2 cups) whole milk
25ml (1fl oz/2 tbsp) dark rum
1 tsp vanilla extract or vanilla bean paste
80g (3oz/⅔ cup) plain (all-purpose) flour
15g (½oz) butter, for greasing
400g (14oz) soft prunes, pitted

1. Preheat the oven to 150°C fan (325°F/gas 3).

2. Combine the eggs in a large mixing bowl with the sugar, then use a hand whisk to mix for a few minutes until the mixture is pale.

3. Warm the milk in a pan, then slowly add it to the egg mixture, whisking all the time.

4. Add the rum and vanilla, then sift in the flour. Stir gently to make a smooth batter.

5. Grease the tin with the butter and spread the prunes over the base of the tin, then pour over the batter.

6. Bake for 40–45 minutes until golden and risen – it will deflate a little as it cools, but don't worry, it should do.

Tips: *Far Breton* is traditionally served cold and set, but I also love it warm, for a creamier texture. Try to buy really good-quality soft prunes for best results.

CRÈME RENVERSÉE

Crème Caramel

A delicate and elegant dessert, *crème renversée* is another French classic that will impress your guests with no effort at all (I promise you!). Maman would make it in a big ceramic tray for us children to dig into with our little spoons. She quickly prepared it in the morning and left it to cook in the oven on a timer before going to the farm. Don't be scared by the word 'caramel', just follow the recipe and be confident! I recommend you make this the day before in some little ramekins so they are ready to turn upside down onto a nice dessert plate for serving.

Serves: 8

Special equipment:

8 ramekins 4cm (1½in) high, a large deep baking tray

Ingredients:

FOR THE CARAMEL:
100g (3½oz/scant ½ cup) caster (superfine) sugar
4 teaspoons water

FOR THE CRÈME:
500ml (18fl oz/2 cups) whole milk (for a creamier version, you could use 250ml/8fl oz/1 cup double/heavy cream and 250ml/8fl oz/1 cup semi-skimmed milk)
2 tsp vanilla bean paste or 2 fresh vanilla pods (don't use vanilla extract, you want the most fragrant vanilla flavour)
2 large eggs and 2 egg yolks
75g (3oz/scant ⅓ cup) caster (superfine) sugar

Tip: To make it even easier, you can prepare this in a large ceramic tray, for everyone to spoon their dessert into individual bowls. This is how we eat it at home!

1. Place your ramekins in the deep baking tray so they are ready to be filled.

2. To make the caramel, heat the sugar and water in a heavy-based pan over a high heat. Use a heatproof spatula to gently stir so that the water 'grabs' all the sugar and makes a white syrup. Leave to cook over a high heat for a couple of minutes – it will start to colour quickly. When you reach that amber caramel colour – 3–4 minutes – it is ready. Quickly pour the caramel into the bottom of each ramekin. Set aside to cool slightly.

3. Warm the milk in a pan to a light simmer (not boiling), then add the vanilla bean paste, or scrape the vanilla pods and add the seeds and scraped-out pods to infuse. Set aside.

4. Preheat the oven to 120°C fan (250°F/gas ½).

5. In a heatproof bowl, whisk together the eggs, egg yolks and sugar for a couple of minutes until combined, then gently stir in the warm milk and vanilla (remove the pods at this point, if using). Pour the vanilla cream on top of the cooled caramel in the ramekins. The creams need to cook in a bain marie, so add warm water to the baking tray, to come one-third of the way up the sides of the ramekins.

6. Cover the ramekins with tin foil so they don't burn on top. Cook for 1 hour 15 minutes. You can check if they are cooked by inserting a knife in the middle, which should come out clean.

7. Leave to cool at room temperature, then cover and refrigerate overnight before serving. To remove from their ramekins, use a sharp knife to go around the edge of the ramekins, place a dessert plate on top, and quickly turn upside down.

CRÈME AU CHOCOLAT ET VANILLE DE MAMIE

Mamie's Chocolate and Vanilla Cream

I have countless memories of eating *crème au chocolat et vanille* with my cousins at my grandparents' farm. They had a dairy farm, so there was plenty of fresh whole milk available for Mamie to make as many *crèmes* as possible. I love how quick and simple this recipe is, but also how rich and delicious a pudding it is. You can make it in a large bowl for everyone to dig in, or in individual ramekins.

Serves: 8

Special equipment:

a large serving bowl or 8 ramekins, a skewer

Ingredients:

FOR THE CHOCOLATE CREAM:
500ml (18fl oz/2 cups) whole milk
100g (3½oz/scant ½ cup) caster (superfine) sugar
60g (2oz) salted butter
200g (7oz) chocolate (minimum 50% cocoa solids)
40g (1½oz/⅓ cup) plain (all-purpose) flour

FOR THE VANILLA CREAM:
500ml (18fl oz/2 cups) whole milk
100g (3½oz/scant ½ cup) caster (superfine) sugar
2 eggs and 1 egg yolk
40g (1½oz/⅓ cup) plain (all-purpose) flour
1 tsp vanilla bean paste or the seeds of 2 vanilla pods

1. If you are making both creams, combine the milk and sugar for both in a large saucepan and bring to the boil, stirring to dissolve the sugar, then set aside to cool.

2. Melt the butter with the chocolate in a bowl using the microwave or a bain marie (see p. 13), then gently sift in the flour and whisk well. Slowly pour half of the milk over, stirring all the while, and return the mixture to the pan. You now have to be patient! Cook the cream for a good 8–10 minutes over a low heat, stirring constantly so the mixture doesn't stick to the bottom. Keep warm until you have prepared the vanilla cream.

3. In a large bowl, whisk the eggs and the egg yolk with the flour and the vanilla bean paste or seeds. Gently pour over the remaining half of the milk, stirring constantly. Return to the pan with the vanilla pod, if using, and cook for 3–4 minutes for the cream to thicken up (remove the vanilla pod, now, if using).

4. Transfer both creams to a large serving bowl, or divide among 8 ramekins, then use a small skewer to marble the two together and make them look pretty. Transfer to the fridge for at least an hour to set.

Tip: You could make just the *crème au chocolat* and add it to little ramekins or yoghurt pots for the family. Children love this recipe!

POMMES AU FOUR

Baked Apples

I don't know whether you can call *pommes au four* a dessert, but it was one of Maman's quick recipes that she made in the autumn using our home-grown apples. I love how caramelised they become on top. You can serve these with some *Crème Chantilly* (Chantilly Cream, p. 171) or it is also delicious with vanilla ice cream and *Sauce Caramel au Beurre Salè* (Caramel and Salted Butter Sauce, p. 175).

Serves: 6–8

Special equipment: a standard baking tray

Ingredients:

6–8 large apples
50g (2oz/generous ¼ cup) granulated brown sugar
2 tsp salted butter

1. Preheat the oven to 220°C fan (475°F/gas 9).

2. Place the apples in the tray, sprinkle with the sugar and dot the butter on the top.

3. Bake in the oven for 20 minutes until golden, remove and allow to cool a little. Serve warm.

Tip: You can also make this recipe with pears or quince for a similar dessert.

TIRAMISU AUX FRAISES D'ÉTÉ

Summer Strawberry Tiramisu

Maman's tiramisu was the first dessert I made by myself at home. This is another of my papa's favourites. Are you starting to understand why I love baking and eating desserts so much? It runs in the family! I can't remember how old I was when I first helped Maman make it, probably around 6 or 7, and my job was to whisk the egg whites with the electric mixer. Over the years, Maman allowed me to make parts of the recipe until I could finally make it all by myself. This is my family's French summer twist – adding strawberries makes it fresher and a bit lighter than the classic Italian tiramisu recipe. This dessert should be made the day before and is a fantastic option for a dinner party. Simply place it on the table for everyone to serve themselves.

Serves: 6 generously

Special equipment: large serving bowl or 6 ramekins

Ingredients:

4 large eggs
75g (3oz/scant ⅓ cup) caster (superfine) sugar
240g (9oz/generous 1 cup) mascarpone cheese
100g (3½oz/generous ⅓ cup) fromage blanc or Greek yoghurt
a pinch of salt
300ml (10fl oz/1¼ cups) freshly boiled water
2 tsp Amaretto (or vanilla extract)
400g (14oz) strawberries
200g (7oz) *boudoir* (ladyfinger or sponge) biscuits
freeze-dried strawberries, to decorate

Tip: To make a classic coffee tiramisu, omit the strawberries and make a different soaking liquor to dip the *boudoirs*: brew 2 espresso coffees and add 2 tbsp of Marsala wine and 200ml (7 fl oz/ scant 1 cup) of water. Then build the tiramisu as above.

1. Separate the eggs between two bowls. Add the sugar to the egg yolks and whisk well for a couple of minutes until pale in colour. Add the mascarpone and fromage blanc or Greek yoghurt and whisk well to combine.

2. Add a pinch of salt to the egg whites and with an electric mixer beat them for 3–5 minutes until they form stiff peaks. With a spatula, gently fold the egg whites into the mascarpone cream.

3. Pour the freshly boiled water into a shallow bowl, then add the Amaretto (or vanilla extract) and set aside.

4. Wash and slice the strawberries (keeping a few to decorate).

5. Start to assemble the tiramisu by soaking one *boudoir* biscuit in the Amaretto soaking liquor for a couple of seconds, then place it at the bottom of a large serving bowl or individually in the ramekins. Repeat with all the *boudoirs*, then once the base is covered, add a layer of sliced strawberries and cover with a layer of mascarpone cream. Repeat with one more layer each of *boudoirs*, strawberries and mascarpone.

6. Cover and keep refrigerated overnight. Serve with some fresh strawberries and freeze-dried strawberries scattered on top.

TARTE MERINGUÉE AUX MYRTILLES

Blueberry Meringue Pie

I didn't grow up eating blueberries – the French don't really eat them. So when I discovered their delicate, unique flavour, I was hooked! This is my twist on the classic lemon meringue pie that we grew up with – another family recipe that Maman made for friends at dinner parties. You can make the pastry yourself or buy it ready-made. Make the base with the blueberry curd the day before and don't hesitate to be extra generous with the meringue on top for an impressive dessert. If you prefer a classic lemon version, I have added the instructions in the tip below.

Serves: 8

Special equipment:

23cm (9in) tart tin, ceramic blind-baking balls (or dry rice)

Ingredients:

FOR THE PASTRY (OPTIONAL):

75g (3oz) salted butter, plus extra for greasing
150g (5oz/scant 1¼ cups) plain (all-purpose) flour, plus extra for dusting
2 tbsp caster (superfine) sugar
½ egg
2 tbsp cold water

FOR THE BLUEBERRY CURD:

250g (9oz) blueberries
180g (6oz/generous ¾ cup) caster (superfine) sugar
4 large eggs and 4 egg yolks
a pinch of salt
juice of ½ lemon
60g (2oz) butter

FOR THE ITALIAN MERINGUE:

160g (5½oz) egg whites
a pinch of salt
300g (10oz/1⅓ cups) caster (superfine) sugar
10 tbsp water

Tip: To make the lemon version, replace the blueberries with 220ml (7½fl oz/scant 1 cup) of lemon juice (about 5 large lemons) and the zest of 2 lemons.

1. For the pastry, mix the butter, flour and sugar together in a bowl with clean fingers until it resembles breadcrumbs. To bring it together, add the egg and cold water. Turn the pastry out onto a well-floured work surface and bring together into a ball.

2. Grease the tin. Roll the pastry out to 3–4mm (⅛–¼in) thick and wide enough to cover the base and sides of the tin, then transfer it to the greased tin. Use your fingers to press the pastry against the base and sides. Trim away any excess with a sharp knife, then use a fork to prick holes on the bottom. Transfer to the freezer for 15 minutes.

3. Preheat the oven to 180°C fan (400°F/gas 6). Cover the pastry with baking paper, then top with a layer of baking balls and blind bake for 15–18 minutes.

4. Meanwhile, make the blueberry curd. Blitz the blueberries in a blender, then pour them into a pan, add the sugar, and heat gently over a medium heat. In another bowl, whisk the eggs and egg yolks with a pinch of salt. Add a third of the hot blueberry purée to the eggs and whisk well, then return the mixture to the pan with the lemon juice. Heat gently for 5–7 minutes, slowly whisking, until the curd thickens, then add the butter, stirring to melt. Leave to cool, then transfer to a bowl and place in the fridge, where it will continue to thicken.

5. Remove the beans and paper from the blind-baked pastry and pour over the thickened curd. Leave to cool at room temperature, then place, covered, in the fridge for at least 3 hours, or overnight if you can.

6. Make the Italian meringue. Place the egg whites and salt into the bowl of an electric mixer. Put the sugar and the water into a pan and heat gently for 2 minutes to dissolve the sugar. Increase the heat to high and cook for 5 minutes, until syrupy. Whip the egg whites to soft peaks with a whisk. Add the syrup and mix for 7 minutes for a thick and glossy Italian meringue.

7. Use a spatula to delicately top the blueberry curd with the meringue. You can use a blowtorch to caramelise the top, or simply put your *tarte* under a hot grill (broiler) for 30 seconds–1 minute.

Fraises
Bois
125g

RIZ AU LAIT DE MAMAN

Maman's Rice Pudding

With my family's access to first-class products, it was always like a little market when we all met for meals and swapped our goodies. Maman freezes milk and primarily makes *riz au lait* with it – it won't be a lie if I say every week. This is a lovely dessert that you can serve with jam or cream.

Serves: 6

Special equipment: a baking dish

Ingredients:

1 litre (1¾ pints/4 cups) whole milk
100g (3½oz/scant ½ cup) Valencia (round) rice
100g (3½oz/scant ½ cup) caster (superfine) sugar
2 vanilla pods, scraped, or 2 tsp vanilla bean paste

1. Preheat the oven to 180°C fan (400°F/gas 6).

2. Add all the ingredients to the baking dish, then give it a little mix with a spatula.

3. Cook for 2 hours – you can cover the dish with tin foil halfway through the bake if it is browning too quickly.

4. Serve warm or at room temperature, with some *Confiture de Fraises de Maman* (Maman's Strawberry Jam, p. 176), *Confiture de Figues (*Fig Jam, p. 177) or cream.

Tip: In Brittany, bakers use the still-hot bread oven to slow-cook the *riz au lait*, which creates what we call *teurgoule*. Try leaving the dish in the oven with the foil on after you have turned it off overnight for it to slow-cook a little more and caramelise.

TARTE RUSTIQUE AUX FRUITS ET HERBES

Fruity Galette

Simpler and more casual than a tart, a galette (*tarte rustique*) means you are not using a tart tin but are free-shaping on a baking tray. I make this galette so often for dinner parties as it's always a success and my friends often ask for the recipe. You can make it with stone fruits as well, or use lavender or rosemary to flavour it – just experiment! Don't forget to add some fresh fruit and herbs on top and serve with vanilla cream.

Serves: 8

Special equipment: a standard baking tray

Ingredients:

100g (3½oz) salted butter, softened
100g (3½oz/generous ¾ cup) icing (confectioners') sugar
1 egg, plus 1 egg yolk
1 tsp vanilla bean paste or vanilla extract
a pinch of salt
100g (3½oz/1 cup) ground almonds
1 sheet of ready-made puff pastry
300g (10oz) raspberries
200g (7oz) blackberries
1 beaten egg, for brushing
2 tsp flaked (slivered) almonds
a couple of sprigs of oregano or rosemary, to garnish

1. Preheat the oven to 190°C fan (410°F /gas 7).

2. In a bowl, combine the butter and icing sugar with a spatula. Add the egg and yolk and mix well in between. Mix in the vanilla, pinch of salt and ground almonds to finish your frangipane. Set aside.

3. Roll out the pastry on a baking tray and spread the frangipane in the middle, leaving a 3cm (1¼in) border around the edge.

4. Cover with three-quarters of the fruits and fold in the sides to make the galette. Use the beaten egg to seal the sides and colour the pastry. Add the flaked almonds around the edges.

5. Bake in the oven for 25–30 minutes, but check after about 20 minutes to make sure it doesn't brown too much – you can cover with tin foil if it colours too quickly.

6. Leave to cool for 15 minutes, then cover with the rest of the fruits and some herbs to serve.

Tip: To make it pretty, I cut scallops with a sharp knife around the edges of the pastry before filling it with the frangipane. I like to serve it warm, with some *Crème Anglaise* (Vanilla Pouring Custard p. 171).

COURONNE COCO AUX FRUITS ROUGES ET NECTARINES

Coconut Savarin with Red Berries and Nectarines

I know all of these desserts are perfect for a dinner party, but this one will definitely steal the show, even for those with full stomachs. It is light, soft and just sweet enough to balance the sharp berries and nectarines on top. This is a gluten-free *entremet* (decorated cake) that you make the day before, then top with fresh fruits before serving.

Serves: 8

Special equipment:

silicon or non-stick savarin mould, a large deep baking tray that fits your mould

Ingredients:

3 large eggs
100g (3½oz/scant ½ cup) caster (superfine) sugar
250g (9oz/1 cup) Greek yoghurt
200ml (7fl oz/scant 1 cup) coconut milk
190g (7oz/generous 2 cups) desiccated (dried shredded) coconut
1 tbsp butter, for greasing

FOR THE TOPPINGS:

300g (10oz) fresh berries (strawberries, raspberries, currants – you can also use good-quality frozen berries in the winter)
3 yellow nectarines

Tip: If you struggle to get the savarin out of your mould, dip it into a tray filled with some boiling water for 5 minutes, then use a spatula to unstick the sides and scrape whatever is left in the mould to shape it again. It is very easy to make it round again and seal it back together!

1. The day before you want to serve it, preheat the oven to 180°C fan (400°F/gas 6). Butter the savarin mould and place it inside a large, deep baking tray.

2. Separate the eggs between two mixing bowls. Whisk the sugar with the egg yolks, then add the yoghurt, coconut milk and desiccated coconut.

3. In the other bowl, whisk the egg whites to stiff peaks, then gently fold this into the coconut batter with a spatula.

4. Pour the batter into the mould and spread evenly. Add some boiling water to the tray, halfway up the side of the mould, and bake for 55 minutes–1 hour. You can check if it wobbles to make sure it is set.

5. Once cooked, leave to cool in the tin at room temperature. Cover and transfer to the fridge overnight to set.

6. Gently use a knife to go around the sides of the mould, place the serving plate on top and then turn it upside down onto the plate (see tip) to release. Wash and slice the berries and nectarines and place them on top or serve them alongside.

CRÈME BRÛLÉE À LA VANILLE

Vanilla Crème Brûlée

Cracking the caramel layer on top of this creamy dessert with a spoon always delights me. Crème brûlée is ridiculously easy to make, very affordable, but oh so chic! A great dessert but it doesn't need too much preparation. You can also serve some raspberries on the side.

Serves: 6

Special equipment:

6 ramekins 12–14cm (4½–6in), deep baking tray for the bain marie

Ingredients:

250ml (8fl oz/1 cup) whole milk
750ml (1¼ pints/3 cups) double (heavy) cream
40g (1½oz) vanilla bean paste or 4 vanilla pods, seeds scraped
9 egg yolks (freeze the whites for another recipe)
170g (6oz/¾ cup) caster (superfine) sugar
100g (3½oz/scant ½ cup) golden granulated sugar

1. Pour the milk and double cream into a pan. Add the vanilla bean paste or vanilla seeds and pods and bring to a gentle boil. Turn off the heat and leave to cool and infuse for 30 minutes. Remove the pods and pour the mixture through a sieve, if needed.

2. Preheat the oven to 100°C fan (225°F/gas ¼).

3. In a glass bowl, quickly whisk the egg yolks with the caster sugar until pale, then slowly pour the warm vanilla milk over the top. Mix well with a spatula.

4. Place the ramekins on a baking tray and divide the vanilla cream among them.

5. Place the tray in the oven, and pour some water into the tray, halfway up the sides of the ramekins, to make a bain marie. Cover the whole tray with tin foil and bake for 45 minutes–1 hour. The *crèmes* should be a little jiggly and the edges cooked. If your ramekins are tall and thick, you might need to add an extra 30 minutes to the bake.

6. Leave the *crèmes* to cool down at room temperature, then transfer to the fridge for at least 3 hours or overnight.

7. Sprinkle a thin layer of golden granulated sugar on top of each *crème*. Caramelise the sugar with a blowtorch, directly burning it to make that satisfying caramel, or put them under a hot grill (broiler) for a couple of minutes for the same effect.

Tip: If you have a blow torch, it is quite fun to do the caramelisation of the crême brulée directly on the table and in front of your guests.

CLAFOUTIS AUX FRUITS DE SAISONS

Seasonal Fruit Clafoutis

I want to show you how versatile this recipe is. It's another standard in both my mamies' homes. They use their homegrown fruits for this, following the seasons. You can make it look more chic by placing the fruit neatly before cooking it, and a final sprinkle of icing (confectioners') sugar or cocoa powder. I love to eat it cold after a summer BBQ or warm with some ice cream in front of the fire after a roast. Here is a base recipe, with my suggestions for seasonal adaptations.

Serves: 6–8

Special equipment:

rectangular tin 31 x 20cm (12 x 8in) or 25–30cm (10–12in) round ceramic dish

Ingredients:

4 eggs
100g (3½oz/scant ½ cup) golden caster (superfine) sugar
150g (5oz/1¼ cups) plain (all-purpose) flour, plus 1 tbsp for dusting
250ml (8fl oz/1 cup) whole milk
60g (2oz) salted butter, plus 1 tsp for greasing

FOR THE SPRING VERSION:
300g (10oz) forced rhubarb
50g (2oz/¼ cup) caster (superfine) sugar

FOR THE SUMMER VERSION:
300g (10oz) apricots
2 sprigs of rosemary

FOR THE AUTUMN VERSION:
1 tsp vanilla bean paste
300g (10oz) figs
2 tbsp fresh runny honey

FOR THE WINTER VERSION:
3 tbsp cocoa powder
50g (2oz/¼ cup) chocolate chips
300g (10oz) pears

1. Crack the eggs into a bowl and stir in the sugar, flour and finally the milk. Melt the butter and mix into the batter until all combined. Set aside.

2. While the batter rests, prepare the seasonal fillings.
Spring: Wash and dice the rhubarb, put it in a bowl and sprinkle the sugar over. Let it sit for 1 hour to allow the juices to come out.
Summer: Wash and destone the apricots and slice them in half. Top with the rosemary before baking.
Autumn: Add the vanilla to the batter. Wash and slice the figs in half. Pour the honey on top of the clafoutis at the end.
Winter: Add the cocoa powder and chocolate chips to the batter. Core and slice the pears in half (you can also peel them, if you like).

3. Preheat the oven to 170°C fan (375°F/gas 5). Grease the tin and dust with flour, arrange the fruits on the base of the tin, and pour over the batter.

4. Bake for 45–50 minutes until golden and set. Don't hesitate to check halfway through and cover with tin foil if it is starting to brown on top.

5. Serve cold in the spring and summer or warm in the autumn and winter with a drizzle of honey or a spoonful of ice cream or cream.

Tip: Any fruit works with clafoutis. You might already know the traditional version with cherries. Mamie also makes it with apples and a teaspoon of Calvados added to the batter.

MOUSSE AU CHOCOLAT DE MAMAN

Maman's Chocolate Mousse

My uncle Jean Charles, chef at his restaurant Le Bretagne in Fougères, Brittany, makes one of the best *mousses au chocolat*. He used to let my sister and I (and my papa) lick the mixing bowl in the restaurant's kitchen before it went to be cleaned! *Tonton* Jean Charles keeps his recipe a secret so Maman developed her own, which is just as good in my opinion.
I think the key to a good mousse is creating a soft and airy texture, but also keeping it rich and creamy. For me, it has to be made with salted butter and have a sprinkling of sea salt on top – trust me!

Serves: 8

Special equipment: 8 ramekins or 1 large serving bowl

Ingredients:

200g (7oz) chocolate (70% cocoa solids), plus 50g (2oz) extra, finely chopped (optional)
75g (3oz) salted butter
50g (2oz/scant ¼ cup) crème fraîche or double (heavy) cream
50g (2oz/scant ½ cup) icing (confectioners') sugar
4 large eggs
a pinch of flaky sea salt

1. In a pan, gently melt the chocolate with the butter, crème fraîche and icing sugar. You can use a microwave to quicken the process (see instructions on p. 13).

2. Separate the egg whites and yolks into two mixing bowls. Add a pinch of salt to the egg whites and whisk for 5–7 minutes until they hold stiff peaks when lifted up with the beater. Set aside.

3. Whisk together the egg yolks, then whisk in the melted butter, chocolate, crème fraîche and sugar mixture.

4. Gently add the chocolate mixture to the egg whites using a spatula, trying not to break up the egg whites too much by folding in a circle, lifting the spatula each time.

5. Add the chopped chocolate, if using, and transfer the mousse mixture to some ramekins or a large serving bowl. Cover and chill in the fridge for at least 3 hours before serving.

Tip: To make it extra delicious, I often sprinkle some Sel de Guerande or Fleur de Sel on top. You could also serve it with some fresh raspberries and crème fraîche.

GÂTEAUX

Cakes

What I love about French cakes is that they are simple, not too sweet, don't have too much icing (frosting), if at all, and are so easy to whip up. Whether you have been asked to make a cake for a friend's birthday (see my birthday cake, p. 64), need an easily transportable loaf cake for a picnic (see the Matcha and Vanilla Marble, p. 59) or just fancy something chocolatey (see Easy Moist Chocolate cake, p. 68) there is something for all tastes. I will also share some alternative flavours and toppings in this chapter – so don't forget to read the tips.

GÂTEAU AUX POMMES ET CALVADOS DE MAMIE

Mamie's Calvados Apple Cake

My Mamie Gilberte makes this cake all the time. She always has some apples in her kitchen, and the rest of the ingredients are just storecupboard staples. Calvados is an apple-based alcoholic drink – a favourite where I come from and very special to me, as my late Grandpa Pierre used to make his own. It is a perfect match with apples, but if you don't have it at home, rum or a little ground cinnamon is just as tasty.

Serves: 8

Special equipment: 20–23cm (8–9in) tart tin

Ingredients:

200g (7oz) salted butter, plus 1 tbsp for greasing
200g (7oz/1⅔ cups) plain (all-purpose) flour (or 120g/4½oz/1 cup gluten-free flour), plus 1 tbsp for dusting
4 medium eggs
200g (7oz/scant 1 cup) caster (superfine) sugar, plus extra for sprinkling
1 tbsp Calvados or rum (optional)
1 tsp baking powder
3–4 cooking apples
icing (confectioners') sugar, for sprinkling

Tip: Mamie likes to serve this still warm, with some of her homemade jam – Rhubarb and Prune (p. 176) and Strawberry (p. 176) work well. I think the Caramel and Salted Butter Sauce (p. 175) is also a great addition.

1. Preheat the oven to 180°C fan (400°F/gas 6). Grease the tin and dust with flour.

2. In a large mixing bowl, whisk together the eggs and sugar.

3. Melt the butter in a pan for a couple of minutes, or in the microwave, then pour it into the egg and sugar mix, stirring until the sugar is melted. Add the Calvados or rum, if using.

4. Combine the baking powder with the flour in a mixing bowl, then add this all in one go to the egg mix. Whisk to create a smooth batter. Set aside.

5. Peel and slice each of the apples into 8 pieces.

6. Pour the cake batter into the tin, arrange the apples on top and sprinkle with the extra sugar.

7. Bake for 40 minutes until golden on top and a skewer inserted into the middle of the cake comes out clean.

QUATRE-QUARTS AU CITRON

Lemon Pound Cake

Quatre-quarts means four quarters, so you use the same amount of each of the four main ingredients. You can weigh your eggs first if you want to know exactly how much of the other ingredients to measure out, but I have made it easy for you here by giving you the weights. This is very similar to a lemon drizzle cake, but instead of drizzle we love to serve it with some homemade jam or to eat with yoghurt for dessert.

Serves: 8–10

Special equipment: 900g (2lb) loaf tin

Ingredients:

240g (9oz) salted butter, melted,
  plus 1 tsp for greasing
240g (9oz/scant 2 cups) caster (superfine) sugar
4 large eggs
zest and juice of 1 lemon
240g (9oz/scant 2 cups) plain (all-purpose) flour,
  plus 1 tsp for dusting
2 tsp baking powder

1. Preheat the oven to 180°C fan (400°F/gas 6).

2. In a bowl, thoroughly whisk the melted butter with the sugar, then add all the eggs, lemon zest and juice, and stir energetically for a couple of minutes to add some air to the mix. Stir the flour and baking powder into the batter until smooth and combined.

3. Grease the tin and dust it with flour, then pour in the batter. With a greased knife, trace a line in the middle of the batter on top of the cake. This will help the cake to rise correctly in the middle.

4. Bake for 35–45 minutes until it is golden and risen fully on top and a skewer inserted into the middle of the cake comes out clean.

5. Remove the cake from the tin and immediately wrap it in cling film (plastic wrap) to keep the steam and moisture inside the cake.

Tip: You can top with some Mascarpone Icing (frosting) (p. 178), or a White Chocolate Ganache (p 179) and decorate with some fresh lemon slices or flowers. You can omit the lemon for a delicious buttery cake.

GÂTEAU AU YAOURT

Yoghurt Cake Four Ways

This is the first cake I EVER baked with Maman. It's very well-known in French households, and it's usually made by little ones using a traditional yoghurt pot to measure out the ingredients. However, *gâteau au yaourt* is not only for small children, so I have added some extra flavours and toppings to tempt all ages!

Serves: 8 generously

Special equipment: 450g (1lb) loaf tin

Ingredients:

BASE RECIPE:
125g (4½oz/generous ½ cup) Greek yoghurt
250g (9oz/generous 1 cup) caster (superfine) sugar
2 eggs
60g (2oz/¼ cup) vegetable oil, plus extra for greasing
225g (8oz/scant 2 cups) plain (all-purpose) flour, plus extra for dusting
1 tsp baking powder

FOR THE CHOCOLATE CHIP VERSION:
100g (3½oz) milk chocolate chips
1 tsp vanilla extract

FOR THE AMARENA CHERRY AND ALMOND VERSION:
150g (5oz) fresh Amarena cherries
2 tsp almond extract

FOR THE ORANGE VERSION:
zest and juice of 1 medium orange

FOR THE CHOCOLATE AND SEA SALT ICING (FROSTING) VERSION:
150g (5oz) dark chocolate (70% cocoa solids)
50g (2oz) salted butter
a pinch of sea salt

1. Preheat the oven to 180°C fan (400°F/gas 6).

2. Put the yoghurt into a mixing bowl, add the sugar and whisk well. Add the eggs, one by one, mixing well in between, then the oil and finish the batter with the flour and baking powder. Mix to a silky-smooth batter.

3. Depending on which recipe you are following, add the flavouring ingredients now.

4. Grease the tin and dust with flour, then pour in the batter. With a greased knife, trace a line in the middle of the batter on top of the cake. This will help the cake to rise correctly in the middle. Bake for 30–35 minutes until a skewer inserted into the middle of the cake comes out clean.

5. Remove the cake from the tin and immediately wrap it with cling film (plastic wrap) to keep the steam and moisture inside the cake.

6. If you are making the chocolate icing, melt the chocolate with the salted butter and simply pour on top of the cooled cake. Sprinkle with sea salt to finish.

GÂTEAU AUX FRAISES

French Strawberry Cake

Probably one of the best and easiest two-tiered sponge cakes, especially if making icing (frosting) or icing a cake isn't normally your thing. I have had great success making this cake over and over, and it has become my husband's family's summer *gâteau*! It also doesn't have to be a tiered cake, as you can fill up a tin or a tray and make one delicious layer. I top it with mascarpone and fresh strawberries – it could not be more effortless.

Serves: 8–10 generously

Special equipment:

2 x 15cm (6in) cake tins, or a 20 x 30cm (8 x 12in) traybake tin, or a 23cm (9in) round tin

Ingredients:

115g (4oz) salted butter, at room temperature, plus 1 tsp for greasing
200g (7oz/scant 1 cup) caster (superfine) sugar, plus 2 tsp for sprinkling
2 large eggs
30g (1oz/2 tablespoons) crème fraîche (or soured cream)
1 tsp vanilla essence
1 tsp baking powder
180g (6oz/generous 1½ cups) plain (all-purpose) flour, plus 1 tsp for dusting
500g (1lb 2oz) strawberries

FOR THE MASCARPONE CREAM:
250g (9oz/generous 1 cup) mascarpone cheese
40g (1½oz/⅓ cup) icing (confectioners') sugar, plus extra for sprinkling
1 tsp vanilla bean paste

1. Preheat the oven to 180°C fan (400°F/gas 6).

2. Cream the butter and the sugar together in a mixing bowl for a few minutes using an electric mixer. Add the eggs, one by one, mixing in between additions, then add the crème fraîche or soured cream and the vanilla essence. Gently mix in the baking powder and the flour to get a uniform thick batter.

3. Grease the tin(s) and cover the base(s) with baking paper, then dust with flour to coat the sides.

4. Keep half of the strawberries to assemble the cake and slice the rest to add to the batter.

5. Divide the batter evenly between the tin (or pour into one), add the sliced strawberries to the tin(s), pushing some slightly into the batter. Sprinkle with the extra caster sugar. Bake for 25–30 minutes until a skewer inserted into the middle of the cake(s) comes out clean. Leave to cool in the tin(s) before turning out and setting on a wire rack to cool completely.

6. Make the mascarpone cream by combining all the ingredients in a bowl. Spread a couple of tablespoons of mascarpone cream onto one cooled cake, then slice a few of the reserved strawberries on top of the cream. Add the second tier and spread with the rest of the mascarpone and top with the remaining whole strawberries. Sprinkle with icing sugar and serve immediately.

Tip: If you actually wanted to make a proper iced cake, I would recommend making these sponges and using the Marscapone Icing (frosting) (p. 178). A fabulous birthday cake!

TARTE TATIN DE MAMAN

Maman's Tarte Tatin

If there is a *tarte tatin* on the menu at a restaurant, you know that is the dessert to order! To me, it outshines chocolate fondant or cheesecake. My secrets for the perfect *tarte tatin* are the salted butter, the apples and how you pre-cook the apples. You have to balance the sweetness of the caramel with the salt of the butter. Choose sweet apples – but ones that keep their shape while cooking, like Braeburn or, my favourite, the Reinette. Maman cooks her apples in the caramel in the oven or on the hob, directly in the cooking tin. You can simplify this recipe by buying good-quality shortcrust or puff pastry rather than making your own.

Serves: 8 generously

Special equipment:

23cm (9in) round tin or tarte tatin dish

Ingredients:

FOR THE PASTRY (OPTIONAL):
125g (4½oz) salted butter, at room temperature
150g (5oz/1¼ cups) plain (all-purpose) flour
1 egg
3 tbsp cold water

FOR THE FILLING:
300g (10oz/1⅓ cups) caster (superfine) sugar
100ml (3½fl oz/scant ½ cup) double (heavy) cream
2 tbsp cold water
100g (3½oz) salted butter
1 tsp salt
8 big apples (Braeburn or Reinette), peeled and cut into quarters

1. If you are making the pastry, do this first. In a bowl, mix together the butter and flour with your fingertips until it resembles breadcrumbs. Add the egg and water, continue mixing with your hands until well combined. Tip the mix out of the bowl onto a clean work surface and shape the mixture into a ball. Wrap in cling film (plastic wrap) and chill in the fridge for 15 minutes before using.

2. Meanwhile, make the caramel. Mix the sugar and the cold water in a pan, and cook over a medium heat for 5 minutes until a caramel has formed. Carefully add the double cream, stirring as you do so. Finish with the butter and the salt, stirring it in well to a smooth sauce.

3. Preheat the oven to 180°C fan (400°F/gas 6).

4. Prepare the fruit. Cook the apples in a pan over a medium heat, adding in half of the caramel and reserving the rest for serving. When they have cooked for 10 minutes (they should be a little bit soft), arrange the apples inside your tin.

5. Roll out the pastry to the size of your tin, then cover the apples in the tin with the pastry, using a fork to prick the pastry so it doesn't rise too much, then cook for 30 minutes until golden.

6. Turn upside down immediately onto a serving tray (see tip below) and serve warm with the remaining caramel sauce.

Tip: Remove any excess juice from the cooked tart before turning it upside down, but reserve it and add it to the reserved caramel. This will give you a lovely sauce to pour over the finished tarte. Serve with some vanilla ice cream or cream.

MARBRÉ AU MATCHA ET À LA VANILLE

Matcha and Vanilla Marble Cake

This recipe combines my childhood and a trip to Japan. *Marbré* is a typical French cake that you will often see at children's parties or at casual home dinners. It is moist, tender and moreish. I was lucky to spend three weeks in Japan some years ago, and I was surprised at how much *pâtisserie* and stunning cakes and biscuits I saw everywhere! There I also discovered matcha, whose strong, bitter, green tea flavour pairs perfectly with the sweet and subtle vanilla bean paste in this cake.

Serves: 10–12

Special equipment: 900g (2lb) loaf tin

Ingredients:

200g (7oz) salted butter, melted, plus 1 tsp for greasing
100ml (3½fl oz/scant ½ cup) single (pouring) cream
250g (9oz/generous 1 cup) caster (superfine) sugar
5 eggs
300g (10oz/scant 2½ cups) plain (all-purpose) flour, plus 1 tsp for dusting
1½ tsp baking powder
1 tsp vanilla bean paste
2 tsp matcha powder
1 tsp olive oil, for greasing

FOR THE CHOCOLATE ICING (FROSTING), OPTIONAL:
100g (3½oz) white chocolate
2 tsp matcha powder

1. In a bowl, combine the melted butter, cream and sugar and whisk swiftly for a minute. Add the eggs, one by one, mixing well in between. Finish by sifting in the flour with the baking powder and briefly mix until you get a smooth batter.

2. Pour half of the batter into another bowl. Add the vanilla to one batch of batter and the matcha powder to the other, mixing each for 30 seconds.

3. Preheat the oven to 180°C fan (400°F/gas 6). Grease the tin and dust it with flour. Pour half of the vanilla batter into the tin, top with half of the matcha batter and repeat. Finally, use a knife to gently dip in and out of the batter about 4 or 5 times, to lightly marble the two flavours together.

4. With a knife, trace a line in the middle of the batter on top of the cake. This will help the cake to rise correctly in the middle. Bake for 50–55 minutes until a skewer inserted into the middle of the cake comes out clean.

5. Leave to cool in the tin for a few minutes, then remove from the tin and leave to cool completely on a wire rack.

6. If you are icing the cake, melt the chocolate with the matcha in a pan or in the microwave in short bursts of a few seconds each time – white chocolate can burn quickly – and pour it over the cooled *marbré*.

Tip: You can wrap the cake with cling film (plastic wrap) when still hot, which keeps the moisture inside the cake while it cools, making it moist and soft for longer.

GÂTEAU AUX ABRICOTS, AMANDE ET LAVANDE

Apricot, Almond and Lavender Cake

Although a cliché, you can't think of the South of France without thinking of lavender. I feel relaxed just imagining its floral and enchanting smell. I came up with this recipe while on holiday with friends in Bergerac, using juicy apricots from the market and lavender from the garden. This is a one-bowl recipe you can easily make while on holiday and can adapt to use any stone fruits or herbs you have to hand (see tip for ideas).

Serves: 8

Special equipment:

a 31 x 25cm (12 x 10in) rectangular baking tray
or a 23cm (9in) cake tin

Ingredients:

100g (3½oz) salted butter, plus 1 tsp for greasing
180g (6oz/1½ cups) plain (all-purpose), plus 1 tsp for dusting
3 eggs
135g (4½oz/¾ cup) granulated brown sugar, plus extra for sprinkling
1 tsp vanilla extract
a pinch of salt
1 tsp baking powder
100g (3½oz/1 cup) ground almonds
80g (3oz/scant ⅓ cup) Greek yoghurt
100g (3½oz/scant ½ cup) vegetable oil
8–10 apricots, pitted
¼ tsp lavender

1. Preheat the oven to 190°C fan (410°F/gas 7). Grease the tin and dust it with flour.

2. In a mixing bowl, combine the eggs, sugar, vanilla and salt. Add the butter, half of the flour, the baking powder and ground almonds, then stir in the yoghurt and the rest of the flour. Whisk in the oil.

3. Dice half of the apricots and thinly slice the rest (to put on top). Add the diced apricots to the batter.

4. Pour the batter into the cake tin and cover with the apricot slices. Sprinkle with the extra sugar and cook for 40–45 minutes. Once cooked, eat immediately.

Tip: Almonds go with any stone fruits, so you can replace the apricots and lavender here with plums and rosemary, peach and thyme or even Mirabelle plums and mint.

GÂTEAU À LA PISTACHE ET ROSE

Pistachio and Rose Cake

Rose is a delicate flavour to work with, but it has a subtle floral touch that's perfect combined with pistachio, and it always takes me back to family holidays in Morocco. We were lucky to spend the weeks with local friends, who helped us discover the best of Moroccan cuisine and especially the local *pâtisseries*. I love this combination, and since I don't like to overpower my bakes with too many flavours (I guess less is more, the French way), we'll keep it simple here.

Serves: 8–10

Special equipment:

23cm (9in) Bundt or cake tin, pastry brush

Ingredients:

220g (8oz) salted butter, at room temperature, plus 2 tsp for greasing
120g (4oz/1 cup) self-raising flour, plus 2 tsp for dusting
200g (7oz/scant 1 cup) golden caster (superfine) sugar
4 eggs
100g (3½oz/1 cup) ground pistachios
100g (3½oz/1 cup) ground almonds
2 tsp rose water
3 tbsp crème fraîche (or soured cream)
1 tsp baking powder

FOR THE ICING (FROSTING):

200g (7oz/generous 1½ cups) icing (confectioners') sugar
1 egg white
extra pistachios

1. Preheat the oven to 170°C fan (375°F/gas 5). Grease the tin and dust it with flour.

In the bowl of an electric mixer, mix the butter and sugar on medium speed for a few minutes until it gets a little bit fluffy. Add the eggs, one by one, using a spatula to scrape the sides if needed. Add the ground pistachios and almonds, the rose water and the crème fraîche or soured cream, and mix again for 30 seconds to combine. Finish by folding the flour and baking powder into the batter.

2. Fill the tin with the batter and use the spatula to smooth the top. Bake for 40–45 minutes. The cake is ready when a skewer inserted into the middle of the cake comes out clean. Quickly turn the cake upside down on a cooling rack, remove the tin and leave to cool completely.

3. Meanwhile, make the icing. Mix the icing sugar with the egg white and add a little bit of water, if needed, to make a thick paste. Pour on top of the cooled cake, then sprinkle with pistachios.

4. Slice and enjoy on its own or with a little bit of cream.

Tip: If you want your cake to have extra green colour, you can add 1 tsp of matcha powder or green food colouring for a more vibrant shade.

MON GATEAU D'ANNIVERSAIRE AU KIWI, NOIX DE COCO ET CHOCOLAT

My Kiwi, Coconut and Chocolate Birthday Cake

When I make this cake, my friends don't really know what to expect. After the first bite I always hear 'Oh wow', 'Mmmm', 'So good' and they are just in love. This is proof that birthday cakes don't always have to be chocolate! It is my brother, Pierre, and my favourite birthday cake, and we both know how to make it ourselves. (He is a great cook!) It is probably the cake with the most flavours in this book, but trust me, it does work and it tastes delicious!

Serves: 8–10

Special equipment: 23cm (9in) springform tin

Ingredients:

140g (5oz) salted butter, plus extra for greasing
240g (9oz/scant 2 cups) plain (all-purpose) flour, plus extra for dusting
240g (9oz/generous 1 cup) caster (superfine) sugar
80g (3oz/scant ⅓ cup) crème fraîche
30–40ml (1–1½fl oz/2–3 tbsp) whole milk
2 large eggs
1 tsp vanilla extract
1 tsp baking powder
100g (3½oz) dark chocolate (70% cocoa solids), melted
5–6 kiwi fruit, peeled and sliced

FOR THE CREAM:

50g (2oz/¼ cup) caster (superfine) sugar
zest of 2 lemons and juice of 1
1 sheet of gelatine
240g (9oz/generous 1 cup) mascarpone cheese
50g (2oz/generous ½ cup) desiccated (dried shredded) coconut

1. Preheat the oven to 160°C fan (350°F/gas 4). Grease the tin and dust it with flour.

2. Cream the butter with the sugar using an electric mixer.

3. In another bowl, mix the crème fraîche, milk, eggs and vanilla extract. Start to slowly add that mix to the butter and alternate by adding the flour and baking powder. Mix well to create a smooth batter.

4. Transfer the batter to the tin and smooth the top. Bake for 35–40 minutes until a skewer inserted into the middle of the cake comes out clean. Leave to cool.

5. Halve the cake into two layers and spread the melted chocolate on the cut sides of each cake layer. Leave to cool and set properly. (You can pop them in the freezer for 10 minutes if needed.)

6. For the cream, combine the sugar, lemon zest and juice and the gelatine in a small pan. Heat over a low heat just to dissolve the gelatine, then leave to cool for a few minutes. Finally, add the mascarpone and the coconut and whisk well.

7. Quickly spread the cream over the chocolate on one of the cakes and transfer to the fridge for 1 hour for the cream to set. Place the second cake layer on top and cover the top with the kiwi slices.

Tip: If kiwi fruits are not your favourite, you can replace them with a mix of strawberries and raspberries, which is also very, very delicious!

GÂTEAU AUX CAROTTES QUE MÊME LES FRANÇAIS ADORENT

Carrot Cake that even French People Adore

When I first told my family about carrot cake, they replied, '*un gâteau aux carottes?*'. They were perplexed. I had to make it for them to believe me! Nowadays there is much more American- and English-style baking in France, but 11 years ago that was definitely not the case! It was the first time my family had had a tiered cake with some sort of icing on top, too. My family love this cake so much now that I made a carrot cake for my parents' 30th wedding anniversary and also one for my sister's 30th birthday.

Serves: 8–10

Special equipment:

three 15cm (6in) cake tins or two 20cm (8in) cake tins

Ingredients:

1 tsp butter, for greasing
300g (10oz/scant 2½ cups) plain (all-purpose) flour, plus 1 tsp for dusting
1½ tsp baking powder
200g (7oz/scant 1 cup) granulated sugar
150g (5oz/generous ¾ cup) light packed brown sugar
a generous pinch of sea salt
1 tbsp ground cinnamon
1 tsp ground mixed spice
100g (3oz/scant 1 cup) chopped walnuts (optional)
280ml (9fl oz/generous 1 cup) vegetable oil
4 large eggs
1 tsp vanilla bean paste
5–6 medium carrots, grated (about 300g/10oz)

FOR THE CREAM CHEESE ICING (FROSTING):

120g (4½oz) slightly salted butter at room temperature
400g (14oz/3¼ cups) icing (confectioners') sugar
220g (8oz/1 cup) cream cheese
1 tsp vanilla bean paste

1. Preheat the oven to 180°C fan (400°F/gas 6). Grease the tins and dust with flour.

2. In a bowl, combine the flour, baking powder, both sugars, salt, cinnamon and mixed spice and stir briefly to combine. Add the chopped walnuts, if using.

3. In another bowl, combine the vegetable oil, eggs, and the vanilla bean paste and stir together before adding to the first bowl. Whisk well until you get a uniform batter. Finish by adding the carrot and use a spatula to blend it in.

4. Divide the batter between the tins and bake for 35–45 minutes until a skewer inserted into the middle of the cake comes out clean. Once cooked, turn upside down on a cooling rack, remove the tin and leave to cool completely.

5. While the cakes cool, make the cream cheese icing. Whip the butter for 2 minutes using an electric mixer, then add half of the icing sugar and whisk for another 2 minutes. Whisk in the cream cheese and vanilla bean paste. Add the remaining icing sugar and whisk for another couple of minutes.

6. Slice the top of one cake with a serrated knife: hold the knife flat and work around the cake to create an even and flat sponge. Use a spatula and spread a 5mm (½in) layer of icing on top of the first sponge. Place the second sponge on top, then spread the rest of the icing on top of the cake (if you have made three smaller sponges, divide the icing evenly among the layers).

Tip: I love how elegant this cake looks with a simple icing and some fresh flowers on top. But you can also keep a more classic look and sprinkle over some extra walnuts.

GÂTEAU SIMPLE AU CHOCOLAT

Easy Chocolate Cake

My sister and I were devastated when Maman bought her first silicon spatula because it meant she could neatly scrape every last bit from the mixing bowls, and there was nothing left to scoop up with our little fingers! We were especially happy when she was making this *gâteau au chocolat*. I now make this myself and can eat as much raw batter as I want! My chic twist on this simple chocolate cake is the addition of dried Amarena cherries and chocolate chips.

Serves: 8 generously

Special equipment:

23–25cm (9–10in) springform cake tin

Ingredients:

200g (7oz) salted butter
150g (5oz) dark chocolate (70% cocoa solids)
4 eggs
200g (7oz/scant 1 cup) caster (superfine) sugar
2 tsp crème fraîche
40g (1½oz/$\frac{1}{3}$ cup) unsweetened cocoa powder
70g (3oz/generous ½ cup) plain (all-purpose) flour
100g (3½oz) milk chocolate chips (optional)
100g (3½oz) dried Amarena cherries (optional)

1. Preheat the oven to 180°C fan (400°F/gas 6).

2. Melt the butter with the chocolate in a pan or in a bowl in the microwave.

3. In another bowl, mix the eggs with the sugar for a couple of minutes, then add the crème fraîche and whisk briefly.

4. Add the chocolate and melted butter mix to the egg mix using a spatula to incorporate it. Finish the batter by sifting in the cocoa powder and the flour. Continue to fold it in until you get a shiny smooth batter.

5. If using, add the milk chocolate chips and cherries, keeping a teaspoon of each to sprinkle on top.

6. Bake for 25–27 minutes – you want it to stay gooey in the middle, so don't overbake it. Leave to cool for 15 minutes before turning out of the tin and serving it warm, or leave it to cool completely if you prefer it cold.

Tip: If you decide to go with the simple chocolate cake (and don't add the cherries or chocolate chips), sprinkle it with some icing (confectioners') sugar and serve warm with cream.

PÂTISSERIES

Pastries

This chapter is all about *pâtisserie*, such as you will find in most *boulangeries* in France. My maman never really bothered making her own éclairs or croissants, we left that to the professionals, and would simply go to the local *boulangerie* every few days to buy fresh handcrafted ones. We are very proud that my cousin Julien, formerly *boulanger* in Paris and now owner of two bakeries in Antibes, won the competition for the best baguette in Paris one year – which is then delivered to the President of France every week!

I taught myself how to master a few techniques from some favourites, and in this chapter I share with you the simplest way to make your own French *pâtisserie* at home. If you feel like trying your hand at choux pastry, I would recommend starting with the *Chouquettes* (Mini Choux Buns, p. 95) or the *Choux à la Pistache et Framboise* (Profiterole filled with Pistachio Cream and Raspberries, p. 75) before attempting the *Mini Pièce Montée* (Mini Croque en Bouche, p. 88), for example. But once you follow the recipe and have made one, it is so straightforward! For special occasions, you have the choice of a beautiful *Millefeuille au Caramel* (Caramel Millefeuille, p. 92), which is uncomplicated and divine, the simpler *Tarte aux Fraises et Crème Pâtissière au Citron* (Strawberry and Lemon Tart, p. 82) with fresh strawberries or a *Tarte au Chocolat Sel de Mer* (Chocolate and Sea Salt Tart, p. 98) for the gourmands.

CHOUX À LA PISTACHE ET FRAMBOISE

Profiterole filled with Pistachio Cream and Raspberries

A twist on the classic *Choux à la crème*, this recipe is a lighter, fresher version. You can flavour it any way you want. I sometimes add a few strawberries or blueberries, or even a dollop of Nutella on the inside for a little surprise!

Makes: 6–8 large choux

Special equipment:

piping bag with 1cm (½in) round nozzle and 2cm (¾in) star nozzle

Ingredients:

FOR THE CHOUX:
150g (5oz/scant ⅔ cup) water
80g (3oz) salted butter
2 tsp caster (superfine) sugar
120g (4oz/1 cup) plain (all-purpose) flour
3 large eggs (have 1 spare egg in case the pastry is too thick), plus 1 egg yolk for egg wash

FOR THE PISTACHIO CREAM:
500ml (18fl oz/2 cups) cold double (heavy) cream
3 tbsp icing (confectioners') sugar
3 tbsp pistachio paste
300g (10oz) raspberries

1. First make the choux pastry: in a pan, heat the water, butter and sugar over a medium heat until the butter melts. Remove from the heat, then add all the flour in one go, mixing with a spatula until it creates a sort of ball of dough. This will take a few minutes. Leave the dough to cool for 10 minutes.

2. Transfer the dough to the bowl of an electric mixer and whisk for 30 seconds. Still mixing, add the eggs, one by one. The consistency will be thick but smooth. Dip a spatula into the dough and it should form a V shape. If it is too sticky, add the extra egg. Transfer the dough to a piping bag with a round nozzle.

3. Preheat the oven to 220°C fan (475°F/gas 9).

4. Pipe the choux: prepare two baking trays with some reusable baking sheets or greaseproof paper. Pipe large 5–6cm (2–2½in) blobs of pastry. Pipe all the choux 3cm (1¼in) apart, then place in the fridge for 10 minutes.

5. Remove the choux from the fridge and brush them with the egg yolk using a pastry brush – this will give them a nice colour when baking.

6. Reduce the oven temperature to 200°C fan (425°F/gas 7) and cook for 18 minutes (do not open the oven door!). Once cooked, turn off the oven, quickly open the door to let the steam out, then close it again and let the choux dry in the oven for another 15–20 minutes.

7. While you are waiting, make the pistachio cream. Pour the double cream into the bowl of an electric mixer fitted with the whisk attachment and mix for a couple of minutes on medium speed. Add the icing sugar and the pistachio paste and whisk on high speed for another couple of minutes. The cream should become thick and pipeable. Fill a piping bag fitted with a large star nozzle with the pistachio cream. Set aside.

8. Remove the choux from the oven, and slice the top off each bun – to make it neat, you can use a round cutter to evenly cut their little 'hats'. Pipe the cream inside the choux to create a lovely shape. Place a raspberry in between each piped cream blob. Place the little choux 'hats' on top and serve.

Tip: You can find pistachio paste in Italian delis, but if not, replace with vanilla bean paste or make the paste yourself by grinding roasted pistachios to a paste in a powerful blender for up to 5 minutes.

GALETTE DES ROIS

Three Kings' Cake

I have eaten a good hundred of these so far in my 30 years of life. In the second weekend of January, the *boulangeries* and shops all over France replace the *bûches de Noël* with the *galette des rois*. The religious tradition celebrates the three kings by adding a *fève* (a ceramic figure, which traditionally was an element of the nativity, but now can be anything) into each cake as an offering. Whoever finds the *fève* in their slice of galette is the king or queen for the day and gets to wear a paper crown. In my family, the youngest person in the room used to go underneath the table and decide which slice went to who, because really, the reason we loved it as children was to get the *fève*! The reason I eat it now is because it is a fantastic frangipane cream set between two pieces of flaky puff pastry.

Serves: 8 generously

Special equipment: baking tray, a ceramic fève

Ingredients:

130g (4½oz) salted butter
80g (3oz/⅓ cup) caster (superfine) sugar
130g (4½oz/1¼ cups) ground almonds
2 large eggs
a pinch of salt
1 tsp vanilla extract
1 tsp rum
2 sheets of store-bought puff pastry
1 extra egg beaten with 1 tbsp milk, for brushing

1. Make the frangipane in a bowl by creaming the butter and sugar together. Add the ground almonds and eggs and mix to a smooth paste. Stir in the salt, vanilla extract and rum.

2. Cut two 20cm (8in) circles of puff pastry using a plate or tin as a guide and a sharp knife.

3. Place one circle of pastry on top of a baking tray lined with baking paper. Spread or pipe the frangipane on top and add the *fève*, leaving 1.5cm (¾in) clear around the edge of the pastry circle. Brush some egg wash around the clear edge of pastry.

4. Place the second pastry circle on top and seal with your fingers. Use a knife to score little marks around the galette (see images, opposite) and brush the galette with the remaining egg wash. Place in the fridge for 30 minutes.

5. Meanwhile, preheat the oven to 170°C fan (375°F/gas 5). Remove the galette from the fridge and brush with more egg wash, then bake for 30–35 minutes until golden.

Tip: If you don't have a *fève*, simply use a large coin, which has been cleaned and sterilised.

MERINGUE FRANÇAISE

French Meringue

I have sweet memories of going to the *boulangerie* and trying to pick the biggest meringue I could see. What often followed after eating that soft sugary cushion was an excess of powdery crumbs around my mouth and sticky fingers – the best part! These are lovely to bring to a picnic, or to make some pavlova on the go; just pick up some *Crème Chantilly* (Chantilly Cream, p. 171), some *Coulis à la Framboise* (Raspberry Sauce p. 172) and fresh fruits for a quick assembly.

Serves: 6–8

Ingredients:

150g (5oz) egg whites (4 large eggs)
a pinch of salt
300g (10oz/1⅓ cups) caster (superfine) sugar

FOR THE TOPPINGS:
cocoa powder
raspberry powder
matcha

1. Preheat the oven to 120°C fan (250°F/gas ½).

2. In a clean bowl, whisk the egg whites and the salt on medium speed for a couple of minutes until the egg whites start to froth, then increase the speed to high and whisk until soft peaks form. Gradually add the caster sugar, using a tablespoon. Mix for at least 4–5 minutes for a glossy and shiny meringue mix.

3. On a lined baking sheet, spoon two blobs of meringue mix and sprinkle one of the toppings on top – you can use the back of the spoon to make a lovely shape with the meringue. Repeat to make 6–8 big meringues.

4. Bake for 1 hour, then leave the meringue in the oven to dry for another 1–2 hours.

Tip: To whisk a perfect meringue, make sure all of your equipment is clean before you begin. You can use a tea (dish) towel spritzed with some lemon juice or vinegar to remove any grease on the bowl or the whisk. One-week-old egg whites at room temperature are best to make a steady and strong meringue.

TARTE AUX FRAISES ET CRÈME PÂTISSIÈRE AU CITRON

Strawberry and Lemon Tart

I make the most of strawberries in the summer, so this is my go-to tart. The lemon *crème pâtissière* gives it an extra zing, making it less sweet than the traditional vanilla version. Top it with fresh mint leaves and daisies, sprinkle some icing sugar on top, and you'll be the queen or king of summer al fresco parties.

Serves: 8

Special equipment:

20–23cm (8–9in) tart tin, ceramic blind-baking balls (or dry rice)

Ingredients:

FOR THE SWEET PASTRY:

100g (3½oz) unsalted butter at room temperature, diced, plus extra for greasing
250g (9oz/2 cups) plain (all-purpose) flour, plus extra for dusting
150g (5oz/1¼ cups) icing (confectioners') sugar, plus extra for sprinkling
a pinch of salt
2 eggs, whisked
400–500g (14oz–1lb 2oz) juicy strawberries

FOR THE LEMON CRÈME PÂTISSIÈRE:

400ml (14fl oz/generous 1½ cups) whole milk
4 egg yolks (freeze the whites for later)
30g (1oz/¼ cup) plain (all-purpose) flour
75g (3oz/⅓ cup) caster (superfine) sugar
zest of 1 lemon and half of the juice

1. You can make the pastry by hand or use a food processor. With clean hands, in a large mixing bowl, crumble the butter into the flour, icing sugar and salt. Once it looks like breadcrumbs, add the whisked eggs and work everything together to create a soft ball of pastry. Flatten the ball on a plate, cover with cling film (plastic wrap) and place in the fridge for 30 minutes or for 10 minutes in the freezer, if you are in a hurry.

2. Meanwhile, make the *crème pâtissière*. Gently warm the milk in a pan. In a glass bowl, whisk the egg yolks, flour and sugar to a pale, smooth consistency. Pour the warm milk over the eggs and whisk well. Return the mixture to the pan, add the lemon zest and juice and cook over medium heat for 3–5 minutes, slowly mixing using a wooden spoon. The *crème* should start to coat the wooden spoon and thicken. It is ready when you obtain a curd or mayonnaise consistency. Transfer to your original bowl, cover and leave to cool.

3. Make your tart case. Dust a clean worktop with flour and use a rolling pin to flatten the pastry to 3–4mm (¼in) thickness. Grease the tart tin with butter and cover with the pastry. Use your fingers to press it against the tin, then use a sharp knife to trim away the edges and make some holes at the bottom of your tart with a fork (this will help it to cook it evenly and not puff up). Place it in the fridge for 30 minutes, or for 10 minutes in the freezer.

4. Preheat the oven to 170°C fan (375°F/gas 5), then blind bake the pastry case with the baking balls for 20–25 minutes. Leave to fully cool in the tin on a cooling rack.

5. Spread the *crème pâtissière* over the base of the pastry and use the back of a spoon to spread it evenly. Place in the fridge while you slice the strawberries. Scatter the strawberries on top and sprinkle over some icing sugar.

Tip: If you have some leftover pastry, simply make some flat cookies and bake them at the same time as the pastry base.

LES CROISSANTS ET PAINS AU CHOCOLAT

Croissants and Pains au Chocolat

This is probably the longest recipe you will find in this book. I guess there are little shortcuts in making croissants, but just like all recipes I have included, read on, follow the instructions and trust the process. You can keep half of the dough in the freezer for up to a month, if you like; just defrost it in the fridge overnight and leave to rise again in the morning in a warm room for an hour before baking fresh croissants from your own bakery.

Makes: 8 croissants and 8 pains au chocolat

Ingredients:

500g (1lb 2oz/4 cups) bread flour, plus extra for dusting
10g (¼oz/2 tsp) salt
60g (2oz/¼ cup) caster (superfine) sugar
100ml (3½fl oz/scant ½ cup) whole milk
125ml (4fl oz/½ cup) water
10g (¼oz/ 2 tsp) instant yeast (25g/1oz fresh yeast)
1 egg, plus 1 extra for brushing
100g (3½oz) salted butter, at room temperature
250g (9oz) unsalted cold butter

FOR THE PAINS AU CHOCOLAT:
100g (3½oz) dark chocolate (70% cocoa solids), sliced into 10 long bars

1. Combine the flour, salt and sugar in the bowl of an electric mixer fitted with the hook attachment. Add the milk, water, yeast, egg and salted butter and whisk on low speed for 3 minutes, then increase to medium speed and whisk for another 5–8 minutes. It is ready when the dough comes away from the sides while mixing.

2. Transfer the dough to another clean bowl, cover with cling film (plastic wrap) and leave to rise in a hot room or until it doubles in size (depending on the temperature, this will take 1–2 hours).

3. Once it has doubled in size, punch the dough down with clean hands to remove the air. Wrap the dough in cling film and place in the freezer for 20 minutes.

4. Lightly flour your worktop and roll a square of dough to 1.5cm (¾in) thick and set aside.

5. Place the unsalted butter on some baking paper, place another piece of baking paper on top, and roll out to a 20cm (8in) square using a rolling pin.

6. Place that butter on the inside of the square of dough and close the dough around it like a envelope, sealing well around the edges with your fingers to keep the butter in. Use a rolling pin to tap it on top and help to seal it.

7. Roll the dough out to a 60 x 20cm (24 x 8in) rectangle, 1.5cm (¾in) thick. With a short edge facing you, fold the top third of the dough back on itself, then fold the bottom third of the dough over to cover it. Give the dough a quarter turn so the opening fold is now on the right.

8. Roll the dough back out to the same size rectangle. Fold the top quarter down and the bottom quarter up to meet in the middle, then fold in half. Cover with cling film and keep in the fridge for 30 minutes.

9. Slice the dough in two – half for the croissants and half for the pains au chocolat. Roll each half out a 70 x 30cm (30 x 12in) rectangle and trim the sides to have clean edges.

10. To make the croissants, cut 8 long triangles along the length of the rectangle, and make a little 1cm (½in) cut at the base of each triangle. Use both of your hands to roll the pastry from the large base all the way to the top of the triangle. Place the croissants on a baking tray lined with some baking paper.

11. To make the pains au chocolat, cut 8 rectangles from the length of pastry, place a bar of chocolate on the edge of each rectangle and fold the pastry over it. Place the pains au chocolat on a baking tray lined with some baking paper.

12. Brush all the pastries with the egg wash, then leave them to rise in a warm room for 1 hour.

13. Preheat the oven to 220°C fan (475°F/gas 9), then cook the pastries for 12–15 minutes, until golden.

MINI PIÈCE MONTÉE

Mini Croque en Bouche

The *pièce montée* for my Catholic communion collapsed at the *boulangerie* before it even made it home. The culprit? The heat! *Pièces montées* are the traditional cakes for any celebration and I chose one for my wedding cake. Imagine a tower of choux in the shape of a tiered cake – it is impressive what you can build with some choux and some caramel. This is the basic recipe you need to make your own little version at home. It does have several steps, but it's worth it to make probably one of the most spectacular cakes!

Serves: 10–12

Special equipment:

2 piping bags with 1cm (½in) round nozzle, a large/pint glass, 2 large baking trays

Ingredients:

FOR THE CHOUX:

150ml (5fl oz/scant ⅔ cup) water
80g (3oz) butter
10g (¼ oz/2 heaped tsp) caster (superfine) sugar
120g (4½oz/1 cup) plain (all-purpose) flour
3–4 medium eggs
vegetable oil, for greasing

FOR THE CRÈME PÂTISSIÈRE:

5 egg yolks (keep 1 egg white for the choux, then freeze the rest)
150g (5oz/⅔ cup) caster (superfine) sugar
100g (3½oz/generous ¾ cup) plain (all-purpose) flour
1 litre (1¾ pints/4 cups) milk
1 tsp vanilla extract

FOR THE CARAMEL:

400g (14oz/1¾ cups) caster (superfine) sugar
2 tsp cider vinegar

1. To make the choux, heat the water, butter and sugar in a pan over a high heat and stir with a wooden spoon until melted. Add all the flour in one go and stir briskly with a wooden spoon until the mixture is smooth and pulls away from the sides of the pan. Remove the pan from the heat and leave the choux to cool in the pan for 10 minutes.

2. Preheat the oven to 200°C fan (425°F/gas 7).

3. Tip the dough (it will have formed a ball) into the bowl of a food processor, then turn it on and add the eggs, one by one – adding an extra egg white if the dough is not runny enough.

4. Fill a piping bag with the choux pastry, and cut the bag open to 1cm (½in) wide. Pipe 2cm (¾in) balls of choux onto a lined baking sheet. Flatten the top of each with a fork dipped in water or egg white so it doesn't stick. Use a pastry brush to brush with egg whites. Bake for 20 minutes, then open the oven door to let the steam out, and close again. Leave the choux inside to dry for 30 minutes–1 hour to cool fully.

5. Meanwhile, make the *crème pâtissière* by mixing the egg yolks with the sugar and flour in a bowl. Warm the milk and vanilla in a pan, then slowly pour it on top of the egg yolk mix, stirring. Pour the liquid back into the pan and cook on medium heat for 3–4 minutes until thickened, stirring with a wooden spoon. The *crème* will start to coat the spoon. Remove from the heat, cover with cling film (plastic wrap) and leave to cool. Once cool, transfer to a piping bag.

6. Make a small hole with a knife at the bottom of a choux bun, and fill it with some *crème pâtissière* – when the choux starts to feel 'heavy' you know it is full. Repeat with all the choux.

7. To make the caramel, combine the sugar and vinegar in a heavy-based pan over a high heat. Once the sugar starts to melt, after a few minutes, leave it to slowly caramelise and turn golden, which should take 4–5 minutes. Tilt the pan on its side for the caramel to stay warm.

8. Dip the top of each choux quickly in the caramel and place them upside down on a sheet of greaseproof paper. It will help to make each bun uniform and look pretty from the outside.

9. Use a tall glass to help you build the *pièce montée*. Grease it with vegetable oil so the caramel doesn't stick to it. Start to build the tower by dipping one side of the choux in the caramel and quickly sticking it to another choux, all around the glass. Be careful as the caramel is very hot and it will act like a glue. Once you have built a couple of layers, carefully remove the glass and finish building the *pièce montée*. Drizzle any remaining caramel over with a fork and decorate with edible flowers, to finish.

MILLEFEUILLE AU CARAMEL

Caramel Millefeuille

Millefeuille translates as 'a thousand leaves' or 'pages', referring to the layering in the puff pastry. In this recipe, we make a rough puff pastry, which is so easy, and makes this pastry less complicated, but which still looks incredible! At home, we usually had the traditional vanilla *crème pâtissière* topped with fondant, but here we are making a caramel version for a delicious twist.

Serves: 8

Special equipment: 2 (or 3) baking sheets, a toothpick

Ingredients:

FOR THE ROUGH PUFF PASTRY:
200g (7oz) unsalted butter
250g (9oz/2 cups) plain (all-purpose) flour, plus extra for dusting
5g (1 tsp) salt
125ml (4½floz/½ cup) cold water

FOR THE CARAMEL:
200g (7oz/scant 1 cup) caster (superfine) sugar
2 tbsp water

FOR THE CARAMEL CRÈME PÂTISSIÈRE:
500ml (18fl oz/2 cups) whole milk
5 egg yolks
70g (3oz/scant ⅓ cup) caster (superfine) sugar
50g (2oz/scant ½ cup) plain (all-purpose) flour

FOR THE ROYAL ICING:
2 egg whites
200–250g (7–9oz/generous 1½–2 cups) icing (confectioners') sugar
1 tsp cocoa powder

1. First make the pastry. Dice the butter and put it in the freezer for 10 minutes.

2. In the bowl of an electric mixer fitted with the hook attachment, combine the flour, salt and the very cold butter. Mix on low speed for 30 seconds just to whisk everything together.

3. Add the cold water and mix on low–medium speed for a couple of minutes. You should still see the chunks of butter (it's important that you do). Remove from the bowl and roughly shape it to make a ball, wrap it with cling film (plastic wrap) and pop in the fridge for 15 minutes.

4. Lightly flour your worktop and roll the dough into a 15 x 50cm (6 x 20in) rectangle (you can use your hands to measure, your hand = the width, your upper arm = the length). With a short edge facing you, fold the top third of the dough back on itself, then fold the bottom third of the dough over to cover it, forming a square. Give the dough a quarter turn so the opening fold is now on the right. Roll the dough back out to the same size rectangle, then fold it in the same way. Wrap in cling film and rest in the freezer for 5–10 minutes. Repeat the rolling, folding, turning, rolling, folding sequence (as above) again, then your pastry is ready. Keep in the fridge while making the *crème pâtissière*.

5. Make the caramel by heating the sugar with the water in a heavy-based pan over a medium heat for a few minutes, then wait a little bit longer until your caramel starts to turn a nice amber colour. Set aside but keep warm.

6. Next, prepare the *crème pâtissière*. In another pan, warm the milk over a medium heat. Add the caramel and whisk well, then gently bring to a boil. In a heatproof mixing bowl, whisk the egg yolks and sugar, then whisk in the flour. Pour the just-boiled caramel milk on top of the egg yolks, whisk quickly, then return the mixture to the pan and cook for 3–5 minutes until you get a thick and mayonnaise-like consistency. Empty the pan into a bowl, cover with cling film and leave to cool and set fully. Keep in the fridge until it is time to assemble the *millefeuille*.

7. Preheat the oven to 180°C fan (400°F/gas 6). Cut the pastry into three, and lightly flour your worktop. Roll the rough puff pastry into three large rectangles (roughly 20 x 25cm/8 x 9in) and 3–5mm (⅛–¼in) thick. Use a fork to prick little holes for the pastry to rise evenly. Bake for 20 minutes until golden and flaky.

8. Time to assemble. Use a spatula to spread half of the *crème pâtissière* on top of one of the pastry layers. Top with a layer of pastry and cover the second layer with the rest of the *crème pâtissière*. Finish with the last layer of pastry.

9. Make the royal icing by mixing the egg whites with the icing sugar. It should be a thick white paste. Reserve 1 tablespoon of the icing and add the cocoa powder to it. Spread the white icing on top of the top layer of pastry making it nice and neat using a spatula. Drizzle lines with the cocoa icing on top of the white icing, then use a toothpick to pull the icing alternately up and down to create the design. Leave to set for at least 3 hours before serving.

CHOUQUETTES

Mini Choux Buns

Last summer, my daughter and I were queuing at the *boulangerie* to get some croissants for breakfast, but Fleur just couldn't resist the sweet smell of the delicious baked foods and was pretty impatient. The *boulangère* saw her and gave her a *chouquette* while she was waiting. Peace at last, thanks to these choux topped with pearl sugar. *Chouquettes* are traditionally served at weddings during the champagne reception, but children love them at any time!

Makes: 24

Special equipment:

piping bag with 1cm (½in) round nozzle, a large baking tray

Ingredients:

125ml (4fl oz/½ cup) water
125ml (4fl oz/½ cup) whole milk
125g (4½oz) salted butter
a pinch of salt
150g (5oz/1¼ cups) plain (all-purpose) flour
4 eggs, plus 1 egg for the egg wash
4 tbsp pearl sugar nibs

1. In a pan, bring the water, milk, butter and salt to the boil, then remove from the heat, add the flour and mix with a spatula. Put the pan back over a medium heat, and slowly cook and reduce the liquid in the batter for 2–3 minutes. Remove from the heat, transfer to a bowl and leave to cool for 10 minutes.

2. Transfer the batter to a food processor or an electric mixer and add the eggs, one by one, mixing in between each addition. The pastry needs to be smooth and quite sticky.

3. Preheat the oven to 165°C fan (365°F/gas 5). Fill a piping bag with the pastry and pipe 2cm (¾in) blobs on a baking tray lined with baking paper.

4. Brush the *chouquettes* with the egg wash and scatter with pearl sugar nibs.

5. Bake in the oven for 20 minutes. Do not open the oven while cooking, only do so once cooked to remove the steam, then close and leave the *chouquettes* to dry in the oven for 30 minutes.

TARTE AU CHOCOLAT ET SEL DE MER

Chocolate and Sea Salt Tart

Another French classic, a dessert for the chocolate-lovers and for those who don't like anything too sweet. It is also a very straightforward and easy recipe, which I find perfect for dinners with friends! You can make it the day before and serve it with some *Sauce Façon Bueno* (Kinder Bueno Sauce, p. 174) or with some *Crème Anglaise* (Vanilla Pouring Custard, p. 171). Don't forget to sprinkle the sea salt on top, it will highlight and empower the chocolate flavours.

Serves: 8–10

Special equipment:

23cm (9in) round tart tin, electric mixer, ceramic blind-baking balls (or dry rice)

Ingredients:

FOR THE PASTRY:

120g (4oz) salted butter, at room temperature
220g (8oz/1¾ cups) plain (all-purpose) flour, plus extra for dusting
100g (3½oz/¾ cup) icing (confectioners') sugar
25g (1oz/scant ¼ cup) unsweetened cocoa powder
30g (1oz/⅓ cup) ground almonds
1 egg
1 tbsp water

FOR THE CHOCOLATE GANACHE:

180g (6oz) dark chocolate (60–70% cocoa solids)
75g (3oz/5 tbsp) whole milk
180ml (6floz/¾ cup) double (heavy) cream
2 eggs
20g (1oz) salted butter
sea salt, for sprinkling

1. To make the pastry, add the butter, flour and icing sugar to the bowl of an electric mixer fitted with the paddle attachment and mix for a couple of minutes, then add the cocoa powder, ground almonds and the egg, and mix again for 30 seconds. Finish the pastry with the 1 tablespoon of water, mixing for 30 seconds and then emptying the bowl onto your worktop. Use your hands to form the dough into a ball, wrap it in cling film (plastic wrap) and place in the fridge for 15 minutes.

2. Lightly flour your worktop, then roll the chilled pastry to a 2mm thickness and to a size that will line your tin. Cover the pastry with some baking paper and fill with rice or ceramic blind-baking balls to weigh down the paper, then transfer to the fridge for 1 hour or the freezer for 15 minutes.

3. Preheat the oven to 170°C fan (375°F/gas 5), and bake the base for 20 minutes. Carefully remove the ceramic balls (or rice) and paper and set aside. Reduce the oven to 140°C fan (325°F/gas 3).

4. Meanwhile, make the ganache. Put the chocolate into a heatproof bowl and set aside. In a pan, bring the milk and double cream to the boil, then immediately remove from the heat and pour straight onto the chocolate. Leave for 1 minute to melt the chocolate, then whisk until you get a smooth ganache with no lumps. Add the eggs and vigorously whisk without adding too much air to the ganache. Lastly, stir in the butter.

5. Pour the ganache onto the cooked pastry base, then bake for 30 minutes. The filling should be firm but with a little wobble. Leave it to cook further if needed.

6. Keep in the fridge for a couple of hours before serving. Serve sprinkled with a pinch of sea salt.

ÉCLAIR AU CHOCOLAT PRALINÉ

Chocolate Praliné Éclair

Another classic *boulangerie* favourite: *éclair au chocolat*. I make mine by some added praliné paste (the same praliné paste made with hazelnuts and caramel as in my *Paris Brest* recipe (p. 106) or one bought from a French deli or ordered online) and ice them with dark chocolate, making them the right nutty sweetness. They are made with choux pastry and filled with a flavoured *crème pâtissière*.

Serves: 12

Special equipment:

piping bag with a 1.5cm (¾in) round nozzle

Ingredients:

FOR THE CHOUX PASTRY:
150ml (5fl oz/scant ⅔) cup cold water
60g (2oz) salted butter, at room temperature
10g (¼oz/2 tsp) caster (superfine) sugar
120g (4½oz/1 cup) plain (all-purpose) flour
3 medium eggs, plus 1 egg yolk for brushing

FOR THE CHOCOLATE AND PRALINÉ CRÈME PÂTISSIÈRE:
500ml (18fl oz/2 cups) whole milk
100g (3½oz/scant ½ cup) caster (superfine) sugar
4 egg yolks
50g (2oz/scant ½ cup) cornflour (cornstarch)
15g (½oz/2 tbsp) unsweetened cocoa powder
3 tbsp praliné paste, store-bought
or make your own (p. 106)

FOR THE ICING (FROSTING):
150g (5oz) dark chocolate (60–70% cocoa solids)
20g (¾oz/4 tsp) vegetable oil
a pinch of salt

1. Preheat the oven to 200°C fan (425°F/gas 7).

2. To make the choux, heat the water, butter and sugar in a pan over a high heat and stir with a wooden spoon until melted. Add all the flour in one go and stir briskly with a wooden spoon until the mixture is smooth and pulls away from the sides of the pan. Remove the pan from the heat and leave the choux to cool in the pan for 10 minutes.

3. Once the pastry has cooled, put into a food processor. Turn the machine on to medium speed, then crack in the eggs, one by one, and whiz briefly to combine.

4. Scoop the pastry into a piping bag with a nozzle, then pipe twelve 12cm (4½in) lines onto greaseproof paper, spaced evenly apart. Brush each éclair with egg yolk, then bake for 20–25 minutes. Leave to dry in the oven for another 10 minutes.

5. Make the *crème pâtissière*: pour the milk and half the sugar into a pan and bring to the boil. In a heatproof mixing bowl, whisk the egg yolks with the cornflour, the rest of the sugar, the cocoa and the praliné paste. Pour half of the hot milk onto the egg mix, stirring, then pour the mixture back into the pan. Cook over a medium heat for 4 minutes, until it is thick and smooth. Pour onto a tray, cover with cling film (plastic wrap) and leave to cool down completely.

6. When the *crème pâtissière* has cooled, transfer it to a piping bag with a small round nozzle. Make 3 little holes at the bottom of each éclair (on the flat side of the choux), and fill them with the *crème pâtissière* until they feel heavy.

7. Melt the chocolate with the oil in a pan or in a bowl in the microwave. Dip the top third of each éclair into the chocolate to coat the top. Leave to set in the fridge for at least 1 hour.

Tip: For an elevated look, sprinkle your éclairs with some chopped roasted hazelnuts.

TARTE BOURDALOUE TONKA

Almond, Pear and Tonka Bean Tart

This might be the most elegant tart there is. Pears are so understated, but they are so tasty. Especially when juicy and paired with tonka bean frangipane! You can find tonka beans in professional baking shops or online. They have such an incredibly sweet flavour, close to vanilla, but more powerful. This is a straightforward recipe and you can use some ready-made short pastry to make it even quicker. It is a great tart to end an autumn dinner.

Serves: 8

Special equipment: 23–25cm (9–10in) fluted tart tin

Ingredients:

FOR THE PASTRY:
100g (3½oz) salted butter at room temperature, diced
2 tsp caster (superfine) sugar
a pinch of salt
175g (6oz/generous 1⅓ cups) plain (all-purpose) flour, plus extra for dusting
1 egg yolk
2 tbsp whole milk

FOR THE ALMOND CREAM:
120g (4oz) salted butter, at room temperature
90g (3¼oz/generous ⅓ cup) caster (superfine) sugar
2 medium eggs
120g (4oz/1¼ cups) ground almonds
½ grated tonka bean
1 tsp plain (all-purpose) flour
4 ripe pears
flaked (slivered) almonds, to scatter
icing (confectioners') sugar, to dust

1. Make the pastry: in a bowl, crumble the butter with the sugar, pinch of salt and flour, then add the egg yolk and milk and quickly mix to form a ball of dough. Don't worry if it is not fully smooth; you don't want to overwork the dough. Cover and put in the fridge for 20 minutes.

2. Make the almond cream: in a bowl, cream the butter and sugar together with a spatula. Add the eggs and whisk well. Stir in the ground almonds, tonka bean and flour, then set aside.

3. Take the pastry from the fridge, flour your worktop and use a rolling pin to roll out a circle of pastry larger than your tin, 3–4mm (⅛in) thick. Gently line your tart tin with it, using your fingers to press it into the sides and trim away the excess pastry, creating neat edges. Use a fork to prick a few holes in the base of the pastry and place the tin in the fridge for 20 minutes, or the freezer for 5 minutes.

4. Preheat the oven to 180°C fan (400°F/gas 6).

5. Prepare your pears. Peel and core them, then slice in half from top to bottom. Slice each half thinly, keeping the slices attached at the base. Place the pears at the bottom of the tin, fanning out the slices, then fill the empty spaces with the almond cream. Sprinkle over some flaked almonds and bake for 35–40 minutes, until golden on top.

6. Serve warm or cold, dusted with icing sugar.

Tip: If you can't get ripe pears, you can use a can of good-quality pears in syrup, which is mostly what the traditional *boulangerie* use.

MERVEILLEUX DE LILLE

Wonders of Lille

Wonders of Lille are one of my favourite *pâtisseries*! Much to my delight, you will find them everywhere in the north of France. I studied in Lille, and it was rare that I didn't stop by a *pâtisserie* to buy one after class. They are made simply with two French meringues sandwiched together with whipped cream and then rolled in grated chocolate or speculoos crumbs (Lotus biscuits). It is like eating a crunchy, soft, sweet cloud.

Makes: 12 medium *merveilleux*

Special equipment:

2 piping bags with 1cm (½in) round nozzle

Ingredients:

FOR THE FRENCH MERINGUE:

4 egg whites
240g (9oz/scant 2 cups) icing (confectioners') sugar
1 tsp cornflour (cornstarch)

FOR THE CREAM:

300ml (10fl oz/1¼ cups) cold double (heavy) cream

FOR THE FLAVOURS:

Praliné Paste (p. 106 or store-bought), speculoos spread (Biscoff), melted chocolate, dessicated (dried shredded) coconut, lemon zest

FOR THE TOPPINGS:

chocolate shavings, chopped nuts of your choice, biscuit crumbs

1. Preheat the oven to 100°C fan (225°F/gas ¼).

2. First make the French meringue. Whisk the egg whites for 2 minutes in a large clean bowl, then start to add the icing sugar, tablespoon by tablespoon. Finally, add the cornflour. Keep whisking for another 5 minutes, until the meringue is thick and glossy.

3. Pipe circles, 3–4cm (1¼–1½in) in diameter, onto a baking mat or a sheet of baking paper, and bake for 1 hour–1 hour 15 minutes. Turn off the oven and leave the meringue inside for 1 hour.

4. Whisk the cold cream in a stand mixer for 2–3 minutes until it is properly whipped and holds, then divide into three bowls. Separately, add 1 teaspoon of each flavouring to each bowl and mix in.

5. Pipe some flavoured cream on top of a cooled meringue and sandwich with another meringue. Add a little bit of cream on top and use a spatula to smooth.

6. Dip the cream-tipped meringue into any of the toppings and serve.

PARIS BREST (my favourite pâtisserie!)

Paris Brest

Anything with *praliné*, I HAVE to eat! This pastry was created in honour of a famous French cycling race, Paris-Brest-Paris, which explains its wheel shape. *Praliné* is made by roasting some hazelnuts, adding them to a dry caramel and finely grating this to a paste. You can simply make it in quantity and keep it for your recipes or buy it from a French shop or online. These Paris Brest are worth the effort.

Makes: 6

Special equipment:

2 baking sheets, sugar thermometer

Ingredients:

FOR THE CHOUX PASTRY:
150ml (5fl oz/scant ⅔ cup) cold water
60g (2oz) salted butter, at room temperature
10g (¼oz/2 tsp) caster (superfine) sugar
120g (4oz/1 cup) plain (all-purpose) flour
3 medium eggs

FOR THE CRAQUELIN:
50g (2oz) butter
50g (2oz/scant ½ cup) plain (all-purpose) flour
50g (2oz/¼ cup) demerera (turbinado) sugar

FOR THE CRÈME PÂTISSIÈRE:
500ml (16fl oz/2 cups) whole milk
75g (3oz/⅓ cup) caster (superfine) sugar
2 eggs, plus 1 egg yolk
30g (1oz/¼ cup) plain (all-purpose) flour
50g (2oz) salted butter

FOR THE PRALINÉ PASTE:
200g (7oz/scant 1 cup) caster (superfine) sugar
60ml (2fl oz/¼ cup) water
125g (4½oz/scant 1 cup) blanched hazelnuts
125g (4½oz/generous ¾ cup) blanched almonds
200g (7oz) butter

roasted hazelnuts and icing (confectioners') sugar, to serve

1. To make the choux, heat the water, butter and sugar in a pan over a high heat and stir with a wooden spoon until melted. Add all the flour in one go and stir briskly until the mixture is smooth and pulls away from the sides of the pan. Remove the pan from the heat and leave the choux to cool in the pan for 10 minutes.

2. Meanwhile, make the *craquelin*. Mix the butter, flour and sugar together in a mixing bowl to form a paste. Spread the paste onto a baking sheet and cover it with another baking sheet. With a rolling pin, roll the paste until it is very thin (1–2mm/1⁄32–1⁄16in) and transfer to the freezer to harden up.

3. Preheat the oven to 200°C fan (425°F/gas 7) and finish the choux pastry. Add the cooled pastry mixture to a food processor, turn the machine onto medium and add the eggs, one by one. Scoop the pastry into a piping bag fitted with a nozzle and pipe 6–7cm (2½–2¾in) circles on a baking sheet lined with greaseproof paper.

4. Take the *craquelin* out of the freezer and cut out 6 circles the same size as the choux, then cover each choux with a *craquelin* circle. Sprinkle each one with some hazelnuts, then bake in the oven for 20 minutes. Turn the oven off and leave the choux inside to dry for another 10 minutes.

5. Make the *crème pâtissière*: pour the milk and half the sugar into a pan over a high heat and bring to the boil. In a heatproof mixing bowl, whisk the egg and egg yolk, then add the remaining sugar and the flour. Pour half of the hot milk onto the egg mix, stirring, then pour the mixture back into the pan and add the butter. Cook over a medium heat for 4 minutes, until it is thick and smooth. Pour onto a tray, cover with cling film (plastic wrap) and leave to cool completely. Set aside at room temperature.

6. Meanwhile, make the praliné. In a pan over a high heat, heat the sugar and the water to syrup, stirring until it reaches 120°C (248°F) on a sugar thermometer and cook to a syrup. Once the temperature is reached, add all of the nuts. Reduce the heat to medium and keep mixing gently for about 7 minutes. The caramel

will start to form, but keep watching it and be careful not to let it burn. Once cooked, pour the mixture onto a sheet of greaseproof paper and spread it out to cool completely. Once cool, transfer to a food processor and blitz for 5 minutes or so until it forms a paste. Set aside at room temperature.

7. Next, finish the Paris Brest cream. The praliné and the *crème pâtissière* need to be at room temperature. Place the 200g (7oz) butter in the bowl of an electric mixer and mix for 5 minutes. Add the *crème pâtissière* and whisk for another 2 minutes, then stir in 100g (3½oz) of the praliné.

8. Put the Paris Brest cream into a piping bag with a star nozzle and cut each of the choux circles in half horizontally. Pipe the cream onto one half of the choux, and cover with the other half. Sprinkle with icing sugar, then decorate with some extra praliné and the roasted hazelnuts.

BÛCHE DE NOËL AUX TROIS CHOCOLATS

Three-chocolate Christmas Log

There is not Noël without a *bûche* – many *bûches*, in fact, in our family. It is the traditional Christmas cake in France, and we stick to that tradition with absolute delight. Mamie Gilberte makes it with a simple salted chocolate *crème au beurre*, and my Auntie Christine makes it with a coffee *crème au beurre* – both are very delicious! My favourite is a three-chocolate version – dark-chocolate *génoise*, white chocolate mousse and milk chocolate whipped ganache.

Serves: 8–10

Special equipment:

large baking sheet, 2 piping bags fitted with 1cm (½in) round nozzles

Ingredients:

FOR THE GÉNOISE:
4 large eggs
120g (4oz/½ cup) caster (superfine) sugar
3 tbsp warm water
90g (3¼oz/¾ cup) plain (all-purpose) flour
15g (½oz/2 tbsp) cornflour (cornstarch)
15g (½oz/2 tbsp) cocoa powder
a pinch of salt

FOR THE WHITE CHOCOLATE MOUSSE:
150g (5oz) white chocolate
250ml (8fl oz/1 cup) double (heavy) cream

FOR THE MILK CHOCOLATE GANACHE (MONTÉE):
300g (10oz) *pâtissière* (or 35%) milk chocolate
260ml (8½oz/generous 1 cup) double (heavy) cream
50g (2oz) salted butter, at room temperature, diced

FOR THE SYRUP:
100ml (3½fl oz/scant ½ cup) water
50g (2oz/¼ cup) caster (superfine) sugar
1 tsp vanilla extract

icing (confectioners') sugar, for dusting

1. Preheat the oven to 180°C fan (400°F/gas 6).

2. Make the *génoise*: separate the egg yolks and whites into two bowls. Add the sugar and warm water to the egg yolks and whisk energetically for a couple of minutes. Stir in the flour, cornflour, cocoa and salt, and mix together with a spatula.

3. Add a pinch of salt to the egg whites and mix with an electric mixer for 5–7 minutes until stiff peaks form. Add half of the egg whites to the egg yolk mixture and whisk well. Fold in the rest of the egg whites gently, using a spatula.

4. Lay some baking paper on a shallow baking sheet and spread the *génoise* over evenly with a spatula. Bake for 10–12 minutes in the oven until softly brown.

5. Cover the warm *génoise* with a clean, damp tea (dish) towel. Turn the baking sheet upside down onto the towel, remove the baking paper, and roll up the *génoise* using the tea towel. Put in the fridge until completely cooled.

6. Make the white chocolate mousse: break the white chocolate into a medium heatproof bowl. Bring the cream to the boil in a pan over a medium heat, then pour over the white chocolate. Gently mix with a spatula until the white chocolate is fully melted. Transfer to the fridge until it is time to assemble the bûche.

7. Next, make the milk chocolate ganache: roughly grate the chocolate with a knife into a large, heatproof bowl. Bring the cream to the boil over a medium heat, then pour over the chocolate and let it sit for 30 seconds. Use a spatula to gently whisk to create a silky smooth ganache, then whisk in the diced butter to melt. Place the bowl in the freezer to set for 30 minutes.

8. Finally, make the syrup: in a pan, combine the water, sugar and vanilla extract and bring to the boil. Cook for 5 minutes until the syrup thickens.

9. When you are ready to assemble the *bûche*, whisk the white chocolate ganache until light and soft using a handheld electric whisk, then fill a piping bag with the mix. Do the same with the milk chocolate ganache in a separate piping bag.

10. Now it's time to assemble the *bûche*. Gently remove the cloth inside the *génoise* and unroll the sponge onto a large piece of cling film (plastic wrap). Use a pastry brush to spread the syrup all over the *génoise*, then pipe the white chocolate mousse on top and roll it up again tightly using the cling film, securing it at each end. Put in the fridge for 15 minutes to set.

11. When ready to serve, cover the rolled-up sponge with the milk chocolate mousse and create a bark effect by drawing lines with a spatula. Decorate with Christmas decorations and sprinkle with icing sugar.

FRAISIER FACILE

Easy Fraisier

It is summer, strawberries are everywhere – time for fraisiers! They fill up the *boulangerie* counters in the summer for good reason. I have simplified mine, using a mascarpone cream sandwiched between two layers of *génoise*. Light on the palate, it is the king to end your al fresco summer party. The colour of the strawberries make it so naturally beautiful, which is why it is important to assemble it properly to get nice clean edges. Don't worry if you get a little extra cream on the strawberries – using a little brush to remove any excess does the trick!

Serves: 8–10

Special equipment: two 25cm (10in) springform tins

Ingredients:

FOR THE GÉNOISE:
6 eggs
140g (5oz/⅔ cup) caster (superfine) sugar
140g (5oz/generous 1 cup) plain (all-purpose) flour
a pinch of salt

FOR THE MASCARPONE CREAM:
240g (5oz/generous 1 cup) mascarpone cheese
500ml (18fl oz/2 cups) single (pouring) cream
100g (3½oz) icing (confectioners') sugar
1 tsp vanilla bean paste

TO SERVE:
200g (7oz) fresh strawberries, cut in half, plus extra to decorate the top
200g (7oz) *Crème Chantilly* (Chantilly Cream, p. 171)
edible flowers (or fresh mint leaves) to decorate
icing (confectioners') sugar, for dusting (optional)

1. Preheat the oven to 180°C fan (400°F/gas 6) and line the tins with baking paper.

2. Separate the eggs between two bowls. Add the sugar to the egg yolks and, using an electric mixer, whisk for 5 minutes, until doubled in size. Gently sift in the flour, mixing it in circles with a spatula. In the other bowl, add the salt to the egg whites and whisk until stiff peaks form. Gently fold the egg whites into the egg yolk, being careful not to knock out the air, to make a smooth, mousse-like batter.

3. Divide the batter between the tins and bake for 12–15 minutes. Leave to cool completely, then transfer the sponges from the tins onto a wire rack. Once cool, trim the sides to create smooth edges.

4. In a bowl, whisk the mascarpone and cream with an electric mixer. Slowly start to add the icing sugar and whisk for 3–4 minutes to get a Chantilly-like texture (it should hold peaks by itself).

5. To assemble the fraisier, place a circle of baking paper or acetate around the edges of the clean cake tin; this will help to retain slick and neat edges. Add one trimmed *génoise* to the bottom of the tin, pushing it down. Place some of the halved strawberries upright and facing out at the edge of the sponge, then spread some mascarpone cream over them to hold the strawberries in place. Add a layer of the mascarpone cream, cover with a layer of sliced strawberries and finish with the rest of the mascarpone cream. Cover with the second *génoise* and press to seal. Refrigerate for 4 hours or overnight.

6. To serve, remove from the tin, and gently peel off the baking paper around the edges. Spread or pipe the Chantilly on top, and add the fresh strawberries and decorate with edible flowers. You could also sprinkle over some icing sugar and top with any remaining strawberries and some mint leaves.

LE GOÛTER

Afternoon Snack

Le goûter is the French version of an afternoon snack, which is ususally defined as an after-school nibble. I have countless memories of getting back from school and feasting on Maman's *Madeleines* (p. 123) smothered with her homemade jam, or toasting *Petit Pains au Lait* (Milk Bread, p. 132) and spreading them with a generous layer of salted butter. We had long school days, because we had to take a bus that took 45 minutes to an hour to get there, driving around the countryside picking up pupils from different farms, so we came home very hungry! *Kouign Amann* (Butter Cake, p. 116) was our ultimate *goûter* when we went on holiday to the Pink Granite Coast in Brittany, and it's a must-try for the butter lovers like me!

KOUIGN AMANN

Butter Cake

This is a traditional pastry from Brittany, which means 'butter cake' in the Breton language. And it is exactly that with a touch of sugar. I'll let you imagine what it tastes like! You can also add some slices of apple, extra caramel or even a sprinkle of cinnamon to give it a twist. Don't be intimidated by the folds and layers, it doesn't have to be perfect and no one will judge your lamination work.

Serves: 8

Special equipment: 23cm (9in) cake tin

Ingredients:

275g (9½oz/2¼ cups) bread flour,
 plus extra for dusting
10g (¼oz/2 tsp) melted butter, plus extra for greasing
4g (scant 1 tsp) salt
7g (2 tsp) active dried yeast
175ml (6fl oz/¾ cup) water
225g (8oz) cold salted butter
200g (7oz/scant 1 cup) caster (superfine) sugar

1. Combine the flour, melted butter, salt, yeast and the water in a large mixing bowl, and knead the dough for 8 minutes.

2. Flatten out the cold butter into a 15cm (6in) square.

3. Place the dough on a lightly floured work surface and roll it into a 30cm (12in) square using a rolling pin. Place the butter square on top of the dough and close the pastry over the top like a pocket. Roll the dough into a long rectangle, approximately 15 x 50 cm (6 x 19¾in) in size. Fold over the top third of the rectangle, then fold the bottom third up to cover it. Transfer to the fridge to rest for 30 minutes.

4. Repeat the rolling and folding technique, but this time scatter the dough rectangle with half of the sugar. Transfer to the fridge to rest for 30 minutes.

5. Preheat the oven to 180°C fan (400°F/gas 6). Grease the cake tin with butter.

6. Roll out the dough to a large rectangle, approximately 40 x 50 cm (15¾ x 19¾in) in size, once more and generously sprinkle with the remaining sugar. Roll it up as if you are making cinnamon buns. Cut the roll into 8 equal-sized rolls, then place them in the buttered tin and cook for 40 minutes until golden.

BRIOCHE FACILE

Easy Brioche

Continental breakfast is how we start our Sundays at home! We each have a favourite *viennoiserie*, mine being brioche. I know it might be controversial, because it is not a croissant, but I can't resist biting into a fresh warm brioche smothered with extra salted butter ... Also, it is fair to say that making a brioche takes a fraction of the time used to make a croissant, so it's definitely one to share with the family and friends.

Serves: 8

Special equipment: a standard baking tray

Ingredients:

250g (9oz/2 cups) bread flour, plus extra for dusting
250g (9oz/2 cups) plain (all-purpose) flour
5g (1 tsp) salt
8g (2½ tsp) active dried yeast
140g (5oz/⅔ cup) caster (superfine) sugar
5 large eggs, plus 1 beaten egg for brushing
15ml (1 tbsp) orange blossom water
250g (9oz) salted butter, diced
1 tbsp of pearl sugar nibs, to decorate

Tip: It does take quite a while to knead your dough, so make sure you follow my timings and let the gluten develop in order to create a soft and elastic brioche dough.

1. In the bowl of an electric mixer fitted with the dough hook, stir the flours, salt, yeast and sugar.

2. In a small bowl, combine the eggs and the orange blossom water, then slowly pour it into the flour mix with the mixer on and knead for 8–10 minutes.

3. Slowly add the butter, cube by cube. Knead for another 8–10 minutes, until the dough is coming away from the sides of the bowl. Leave at room temperature to rise for 2–3 hours.

4. Weigh out 8 balls, 100g (3½oz) each. Roll the rest of the dough on a lightly floured work surface to make a large circle of about 30cm (12in) diameter. Place the 8 balls on top around the edge of the circle of dough. Slice a star shape in the centre of the circle of dough, from one side of a ball to the other side of the ball opposite. This will create one triangle of dough per ball. Fold each triangle over each ball, covering part of it. Trim the outside of the circle to make a neat, uniform edge. Leave to rise for 1 hour.

5. Preheat the oven to 180°C fan (400°F/gas 6), and set a bowl of water on the bottom of the oven.

6. Brush the brioche with the egg wash and scatter with pearl sugar nibs.

7. Bake for 25–30 minutes and enjoy warm.

BRIOCHE TRESSÉE AUX MYRTILLES

Blueberry Brioche Swirl

I love to make this centrepiece when friends join me for breakfast! I always asked my papa to pick brioche for me when he was on the *viennoiserie* run to the *boulangerie* on Sunday mornings. This *Brioche Tressée* looks really impressive in the middle of the table, and I serve it with some homemade jams or simply butter. It's also great sliced and toasted the next day.

Serves: 8–10 generously

Special equipment:

large baking tray or 30cm (12in) springform cake tin

Ingredients:

500g (1lb 2oz/4 cups) bread flour,
plus extra for dusting
100g (3½oz/scant ½ cup) caster (superfine) sugar
10g (¼oz/2 tsp) salt
9g (1 tbsp) instant yeast
6 eggs
250g (9oz) salted butter, diced, plus extra for greasing
zest of 1 lemon

FOR THE BLUEBERRY JAM:
100g (3½oz/⅔ cup) blueberries
100g (3½oz/scant ½ cup) caster (superfine) sugar

1. Combine the flour, sugar, salt and yeast in the bowl of an electric mixer fitted with the dough hook. Mix for 30 seconds to combine, then add all the eggs and mix for 5 minutes on low speed, then for another 5 minutes on medium speed.

2. Add the butter one cube at a time (this should take a few minutes). The dough is ready when it is coming away from the sides of the bowl, probably another 5 minutes on low-medium speed.

3. Cover the bowl with a damp tea (dish) towel and leave to rise for 2 hours at room temperature.

4. In the meantime, add the blueberries and sugar to a pan with a couple of tablespoons of water. Bring to the boil and use a fork to mash the blueberries. Let it simmer for 5 minutes, then remove from the heat and leave to cool down and thicken.

5. When the brioche dough is ready, lightly flour a worktop and create a large rectangle with the dough. Spread the jam across the dough. Roll the dough into a Swiss roll and transfer to the fridge for 30 minutes to firm up.

6. Grease the tin with butter. Take the roll out of the fridge and use a sharp knife to halve the roll lengthways. Carefully twist the two pieces of roll together, gently stretching it if needed. Once you have a long twist, place it in the greased tin and seal the edges together with your fingers. Leave to rise for 1 hour.

7. Preheat the oven to 180°C fan (400°F/gas 6), then bake for 35–40 minutes until fully cooked. Make sure you cover the brioche with tin foil halfway through the baking time to prevent it burning. You will get a golden and plump brioche.

8. Enjoy warm on its own or toasted and spread with more jam.

MADELEINES QUATRE FAÇONS

Madeleines Four Ways

These classic French scalloped mini cakes are loved by people of all ages. I think there is something quite special about the way they look, and they are always impressive to serve. We eat them for *le goûter* or with coffee, always shared with friends or family.

Makes: 24 madeleines or 48 mini madeleines

Special equipment:

2 x 12-hole madeleine moulds, a toothpick or sharp knife

Ingredients:

3 large eggs
200g (7oz/scant 1 cup) caster (superfine) sugar
250g (9oz/2 cups) plain (all-purpose) flour, plus 2 tbsp for dusting
1½ tsp baking powder
125g (4½oz) salted butter, melted, plus 2 tbsp for greasing
50ml (2fl oz/3 tbsp) whole milk

FOR THE FLAVOURINGS:

zest of 1 lemon
30g (1oz) freeze-dried raspberries
1 tsp vanilla extract
Nutella
200g (7oz) white chocolate

Tip: It is essential you leave your batter to rest; if not, you are risking the madeleines not rising properly and having a bump.

1. In a bowl, whisk the eggs with the sugar for a couple of minutes. Sift in the flour and baking powder. Add the melted butter and whisk well. Finish the batter with the milk and whisk until smooth and thick.

2. If you are making the lemon madeleines, add the zest of a lemon to the batter. If you are making marbled madeleines, separate the batter between two bowls. Add some freeze-dried raspberries to one bowl of batter and 1 teaspoon of vanilla extract to the other bowl of batter. Cover and leave to rest for at least 1 hour or overnight in the fridge.

3. Preheat the oven to 220°C fan (475°F/gas 9). Grease the madeleine moulds with butter using a pastry brush and dust with flour.

For lemon madeleines, fill the moulds up to three-quarters full, using either a spoon or a piping bag. For the marbled ones, spoon or pipe equal parts of the raspberry and vanilla batter into each mould, until it's three-quarters full. Marble the batter by dragging a toothpick or a sharp knife through the two batters to create a swirl.

4. If you are making mini madeleines, bake them for 6 minutes, then reduce the temperature to 200°C fan (425°F/gas 7) and cook for a further 2 minutes. If you are making large madeleines, bake for 6 minutes, then reduce the temperature to 200°C (425°F/gas 7) and cook for a further 4 minutes.

5. Once the madeleines have cooled down, you could try either of these chocolate variations. For Nutella-filled madeleines, fill a piping bag fitted with a round nozzle with Nutella and fill the madeleine from the bottom. If you would like chocolate-coated madeleines, melt 200g (7oz) of white chocolate using a bain-marie or microwave. Clean the moulds (this works much better with silicon moulds), then pour some chocolate into each hole and immediately put a madeleine on top and press gently. Leave the chocolate to set completely for 1 hour in the fridge, then gently remove them from the moulds with the chocolate coating in place.

CRÊPES

Pancakes

I don't think I really need to say much to introduce this recipe! Being from Brittany, crêpes are a regional dish. I grew up eating them (and the savoury version, galettes) every single Friday – and still do now. If you come to my home on a Friday, you know that you are going to eat some galettes and crêpes – my absolute joy! I don't think you can get bored of them, or maybe that is the Bretonne in me. They are, of course, every kid's favourite, and perfect for little hungry stomachs. See the *Petits Extras* chapter (Accompaniments, p. 167) for some ideas for fillings.

Makes: 14 crêpes

Special equipment:

a crêpe pan or non-stick 24cm (9in) frying pan (skillet)

Ingredients:

250g (9oz/2 cups) plain (all-purpose) flour
4 tbsp caster (superfine) sugar
a pinch of salt
500ml (18fl oz/2 cups) milk
50g (2oz) salted butter, melted
4 eggs
4 tbsp vegetable oil

1. Combine the flour, sugar and salt in a large mixing bowl. Gently pour in the milk and whisk it into the flour. Add the melted butter and whisk well, then whisk in the eggs.

2. Cover and leave the batter to rest at room temperature for 30 minutes–1 hour before cooking the crêpes.

3. Grease a crêpe pan with some of the vegetable oil, and place it over a high heat. With a ladle, pour some batter into the pan, and cook for 1–2 minutes on each side. Repeat until all the batter is used, adding a little more oil if needed.

4. Eat the crêpes straight away, or keep warm, placing a piece of greaseproof paper between each one.
If you are reheating the crêpes, heat them with a bit of butter in the pan for the best flavour. I like to serve these with some *Coulis au Chocolat* (Chocolate Sauce, p. 172) or some *Sauce Façon Bueno* (Kinder Bueno Sauce, p. 174).

Tip: For even nicer crêpes, you can make the batter the day before and store it in the fridge overnight, ready for the morning.

FAUX PAIN AU LEVAIN RAPIDE

Cheat's Overnight Sourdough

If making bread is not usually your thing, this is for you. Because let's be honest, there is nothing nicer than warm, freshly homemade bread, slathered with a thick layer of cold salted butter. I make this using a big pan that I seal and cook the bread inside, to give it a crisp and beautiful crust.

Makes: 1 medium loaf

Special equipment:

clean tea (dish) towel, a large ovenproof pan with a lid

Ingredients:

450g (16oz/scant 3⅔ cups) bread flour, plus extra for dusting
1 tsp dried yeast
1 tsp salt
320ml (11oz/1⅓ cups) warm water

Tip: If you need to use a generous amount of flour to manipulate the dough, don't hesitate as it will be very sticky.

1. In a large mixing bowl, combine all the ingredients using a spatula to make a uniform sticky dough. Cover the bowl with a damp cloth or cling film (plastic wrap) and leave overnight at room temperature.

2. The next day, preheat the oven to 240°C fan (500°F/gas 10).

3. Sprinkle a handful of flour onto a sheet of baking paper. Flour your hands and form a ball with the dough, then place it on top of the baking paper and transfer both the paper and the dough to a large pan.

4. Cover the pan with the lid and bake for 30 minutes with the lid on, then remove the lid and cook for another 25 minutes. The bread is cooked when you tap the base of the loaf and it sounds hollow.

BEIGNETS DE MAMIE

Mamie's Beignets

'*Une poignée de farine par oeuf et du lait*' – 'A handful of flour for each egg and some milk'– is the recipe my Mamie Suzanne gave to me when I asked her how she made her beignets. I had to try it a couple of times to get it right by her. We sometimes had a beignets evening at Mamie's, when the only thing we ate were these apples wrapped in a light, deep-fried dough.

Serves: 4

Ingredients:

4 eggs
4 tsp caster (superfine) sugar
120g (4½oz/1 cup) plain (all-purpose) flour
1–2 tsp baking powder
1 tbsp whole milk
1 tsp rum, Calvados or Amaretto
1 litre (1¾ pints/4 cups) vegetable oil
4 apples, peeled, cored and sliced into circles
100g (3½oz/generous ¾ cup) icing (confectioners') sugar

Tip: Mamie told me to tell you that she whips the egg whites and adds them to the batter at the last minute, right before deep-frying the beignets, so the batter is fresh.

1. To make the beignet batter, separate the eggs into two clean bowls. Add the sugar to the egg yolks and whisk well, then add the flour, baking powder, milk and rum, and whisk again to a smooth batter.

2. When you are ready to make the beignets, whisk the egg whites to soft peaks, then gently fold them into the batter.

3. Heat the oil to 150–170°C (65–76°F) in a large pan or wok.

4. Use a fork to dip the apple slices into the batter and carefully add to the oil, frying on each side for a couple of minutes until they get that nice brown colour.

5. Sprinkle with icing sugar and serve immediately.

BROWNIE AU CHOCOLAT KINDER

Kinder Brownies

My brother, sister and I used to be given one Kinder Egg a week by our childminder, and even now my husband knows what to do if he needs to cheer me up! If you are looking for a brownie recipe to make over and over again, to me, this is the one. The dark chocolate of the brownie is balanced with the sweetness of the milk-and-white-chocolate Kinder Chocolate bar.

Serves: 10–12

Special equipment: 30cm (12in) brownie or baking tin

Ingredients:

185g (6½oz) salted butter, plus extra for greasing
3 large eggs
275g (9½oz/scant 1¼ cups) golden caster (superfine) sugar
185g (6½oz) dark chocolate (60–70% cocoa solids)
40g (1½oz/⅓ cup) cocoa powder
85g (3oz/⅔ cup) plain (all-purpose) flour, plus extra for dusting
8 big Kinder Chocolate bars

1. Preheat the oven to 170°C fan (375°F/gas 5). Grease and dust the baking tin.

2. Using a hand-held electric mixer, combine the eggs and the sugar in a heatproof mixing bowl.

3. Melt the chocolate and butter in a bowl in the microwave or in a pan, then add to the egg and sugar mix. Stir in the cocoa and flour to combine.

4. Cut the Kinder Chocolate bars into small pieces and add to the mix, then pour the batter into the baking tin.

5. Cook for 25–30 minutes until a skewer inserted into the middle of the cake comes out clean. Leave to cool in the tin, before turning out onto a wire rack. Serve warm or cold.

Tip: If Kinder bars are not a favourite of yours, you can just replace them with white chocolate chips and milk chocolate chips, or your preferred chocolate bar.

PETIT PAINS AU LAIT

Milk Bread

Walking back from our school bus, my sister and I had to walk pass the *boulangerie* in our village that made the BEST *petit pains au lait*. They were hard to resist, so our pocket money was always well spent there. It is a perfect *goûter* on its own, but you can also have it for breakfast dipped in chocolate milk, or sliced in two and spread with some salted butter and jam. I love these plain, but your children may like them more with some chocolate!

Serves: 10

Ingredients:

500g (1lb 2oz/4 cups) white bread flour
10g (¼oz/2 tsp) salt
50g (2oz/¼ cup) caster (superfine) sugar
2 eggs, plus 1 extra egg for the egg wash
10g (¼oz/2 tsp) honey
7g (2 tsp) dried yeast (or 15g/1oz fresh yeast)
200ml (7fl oz/scant 1 cup) whole milk
100g (3½oz) salted butter, diced
100g (3½oz) chocolate chips (optional)
150g (5oz) pearl sugar nibs (optional)

Tip: To create a proving oven, put a bowl of just-boiled water on the base of the oven and place your dough on a baking sheet above it. The humidity will help, as will the heat. You can also preheat your oven to 50°C fan (122°F/gas ¼), then turn it off when placing the dough inside. Try not to make it too warm; leave the door of the oven open at the beginning while the oven still retains some heat.

1. Put the flour, salt, sugar, eggs, honey, yeast, and finally the milk in the bowl of an electric mixer fitted with the dough hook. Mix on low speed for 5 minutes to blend everything together. Increase the speed to medium and leave it to knead for another 5 minutes, then add the butter, a couple of cubes at a time, still mixing on medium speed.

2. Increase the speed a little to knead the dough until it becomes more elastic. The ball of dough will start to form a ball around the hook.

3. Remove the dough from the hook and shape it into a neat ball, transfer to a mixing bowl and cover with a damp cloth or cling film (plastic wrap). Leave at room temperature for 1 hour to prove.

4. After an hour, punch the dough to disperse some of the air bubbles and reshape it into a ball. Transfer to the fridge for 30 minutes. (You can add the chocolate chips at this point, if using.)

5. It is time to make your little *pains*! Take a handful of dough (about 80–100g/3–3½oz) and start to form into a ball, pressing the dough in your palm against the worktop in a circular motion. Once you have a nice ball, roll it to create a mini baguette, then place on a baking tray lined with baking paper. Repeat with the rest of the dough.

6. Use a pastry brush to brush the egg wash over each *petit pain* so they will have a golden colour after baking.

7. Leave to rise for 2 hours in a warm room or in a warm oven (see tip).

8. Preheat the oven to 180°C fan (400°F/gas 6) and brush the *pains* with some more egg wash. Dip some scissors in cold water and gently slice the sides of the rolls to create little spikes for a traditional look. You can also put some pearl sugar nibs on top, if you like.

9. Reduce the oven to 170°C fan (375°F/gas 5) and cook for 12 minutes until golden.

GAUFRES

Waffles

I have so many memories of eating *gaufres* as a child on holidays by the sea or at home with my friends on Wednesdays. These waffles are fluffy, light and crispy. I like to make them for my friends for brunch; I think it makes the whole spread a bit more interesting and it is quite a treat! You can easily eat them with *Confiture De Figues* (Fig Jam, p. 177), topped with vanilla *Crème Chantilly* (Chantilly Cream, p. 171), or try a savoury version with some lemon cream cheese and smoked salmon, or with an egg as your own *gaufre royale*.

Makes: 12 large waffles

Special equipment: waffle maker

Ingredients:

300ml (10fl oz/1¼ cups) milk
100g (3½oz) salted butter
250g (9oz/2 cups) plain (all-purpose) flour
1 tsp baking powder
70g (3oz/scant ⅓ cup) caster (superfine) sugar
¼ tsp salt
2 eggs and 3 egg whites

Tip: You can make the batter the night before and it will be perfect for the next morning.

1. In a pan over a medium heat, gently heat the milk with the butter until it has melted.

2. In a large mixing bowl, combine the flour, baking powder, sugar and salt, then whisk in the eggs and egg whites.

3. Finally, add the melted butter and milk and stir to a smooth batter.

4. Heat the waffle maker and once hot add the batter – there's no extra grease needed – and cook for 3–4 minutes until golden.

ET VOILÀ!

CHARLOTTE AUX FRAISES

Strawberry Charlotte

Boudoir biscuits were originally created for Marie Antoinette, who is supposed to have said, 'Let them eat cake'! A light strawberry mousse with a circle of *boudoirs* all around the side, this looks very elegant and pretty. Make sure you prepare it the day before and keep it in the fridge overnight for it to set correctly.

Serves: 6–8

Special equipment:

18 or 20cm (7 or 8in) springform tin

Ingredients:

500g (1lb 2oz) strawberries)
200ml (7fl oz/scant 1 cup) just-boiled water
150g (5oz/⅔ cup) caster (superfine) sugar
1 tbsp butter, for greasing
1 tsp vanilla extract
1 pack of *boudoir* (ladyfinger or sponge) biscuits
300ml (10fl oz/1¼ cups) double (heavy) cream
squeeze of lemon
3–4 sheets of gelatine (or agar agar)

1. Purée 400g (14oz) of the strawberries in a food processor or using a bowl and fork, and set aside 6 or 7 whole strawberries to use as decoration.

2. Make a syrup with the just-boiled water and half of the sugar. Heat over a high heat in a pan until the sugar dissolves, then add the vanilla extract and remove from the heat.

3. Grease the tin with a little butter, then dip your biscuits one by one in the syrup, and place them upright around the edge of the tin. Set aside.

4. Make a Chantilly with the double cream by whisking it in a stand mixer, then whisk in the rest of the sugar and the lemon juice.

5. Place the gelatine sheets in a bowl of warm water for 5 minutes to rehydrate, then squeeze out the excess water and stir the sheets into the still-warm syrup until they have dissolved. Pour the syrup into the strawberry purée and stir to combine. Add the Chantilly and stir in.

6. Assemble the Charlotte: spread some of the strawberry mousse at the bottom and cover with slices of the reserved strawberries. Repeat these layers a couple of times until you reach the top of the tin. Leave in the fridge overnight to set. Serve cold.

Tip: I like to tie a large ribbon around the Charlotte just before serving it.

BONBONS & BISCUITS

Sweets & Biscuits

This is something I get from Maman; we have a drawer at home where she keeps her bonbons and biscuits, homemade but sometimes store-bought from local artisans, ready for the many friends they have over for a coffee or a soft drink. It is very common in my hometown to just drop by, uninvited, to come to say hi and catch up.

This chapter is full of little gems, plenty of well-known French biscuits and bonbons you might have seen in France. All of them can be wrapped up in little bags to make the perfect homemade gift.

FINANCIERS AU BEURRE NOISETTE

Brown Butter Financiers

I remember making financiers with Maman, eating them warm just after they'd come out of the oven. These little cakes are nutty, buttery and will keep for quite some time, so they are the perfect little delicacy to give to friends or to bring to a picnic. They are also really simple to make.

Makes: 12 financiers

Special equipment:

mini muffin moulds or classic *financier* moulds

Ingredients:

140g (5oz) salted butter
150g (5oz/1½ cups) ground almonds
150g (5oz/scant 1¼ cups) icing (confectioners') sugar
50g (2oz/scant ½ cup) plain (all-purpose) flour
3 egg whites

Tip: For a pistachio version, add 20g (¾oz/2 tbsp) ground pistachios to the batter, then top with extra crushed pistachios before baking.

1. Preheat the oven to 200°C fan (425°F/gas 7).

2. Melt the butter in a pan and leave it for 5 minutes, until you get a nutty brown colour. Pour into a bowl and leave to cool a little.

3. In a bowl, whisk together the ground almonds, icing sugar, flour and egg whites, then stir in the cooled brown butter.

4. Fill the greased moulds three-quarters full with the batter and bake for 15 minutes.

CARAMEL AU BEURRE SALÉ

Sea Salt Caramel Bonbons

Being from Brittany, *caramel au beurre salé* runs in my blood! You can find these bonbons everywhere in the region, and this is a simple recipe for you to make at home. We eat these after a meal or with a coffee. They also make a lovely homemade gift.

Makes: 12 bonbons

Special equipment: a standard baking tray

Ingredients:

180ml (6fl oz/¾ cup) double (heavy) cream
180g (6oz/generous ¾ cup) caster (superfine) sugar
50g (2oz/2 tbsp) clear honey
50g (2oz) salted butter
1 tsp flaked sea salt

1. Line the baking tray with some baking paper.

2. In a pan over a high heat, bring the double cream to the boil, then add the sugar and honey. Turn down the heat and leave it to simmer for 10 minutes.

3. Remove from the heat and add the salted butter, stirring to melt and combine. Pour this caramel on top of the baking paper to form a thick 2cm (¾in) rectangle layer.

4. Leave to cool completely (at least 4 hours), then cut into small 3 x 2cm (1¼ x ¾in) rectangles. Sprinkle with sea salt and wrap each one in baking paper to make bonbons.

5. Store in an airtight tin and eat within a couple of weeks.

MACARONS

Macarons

My papa used to buy us each a kilo of fresh macarons for our birthdays. I remember how we had to share our present with the rest of the family, but what a treat it was to have a few macarons every night after dinner! My parents have an egg farm and they supplied egg whites for the *pâtissier/chocolatier* who made these macarons. We also fought to go on delivery with my papa when he was going to drop off the egg whites, because the lovely baker always gave us the misshaped macarons of the day to take home. This is the basic macarons recipe.

Makes: 24

Special equipment:

sugar thermometer, 4 standard baking trays, 2 large piping bags, 1 cm (½in) round nozzle

Ingredients:

150g (5oz/1½ cups) ground almonds
150g (5oz/1¼ cups) icing (confectioners') sugar
110g (4oz) egg whites at room temperature, divided
150g (5oz/⅔ cup) caster (superfine) sugar
50ml (2fl oz/3 tbsp) water
1 tbsp vanilla extract

FOR THE CHOCOLATE GANACHE:
65ml (2½fl oz/¼ cup) double (heavy) cream
200g (7oz) dark chocolate (60–70% cocoa solids), broken into squares
½ tsp salt

1. Combine the ground almonds and icing sugar and 55g (2oz) of the egg whites. Mix until it forms a paste, then set aside.

2. Put the remaining 55g (2oz) of egg whites into the bowl of an electric mixer and start to whisk until the mixture forms soft peaks.

3. In a pan, heat the caster sugar and the water over a medium heat until the sugar has dissolved. Cook until it reaches 118°C (244°F) on a sugar thermometer. Slowly pour the syrup into the beaten egg whites, mixing as you do so. Leave the meringue mix to cool and reach room temperature – about 8–10 minutes.

4. When the Italian meringue has cooled, add 4 tablespoons to the almond paste, then add the vanilla extract and mix well to a smooth texture. Add the remaining Italian meringue to the paste and stir for about 5 minutes. You need to get a soft mix but not liquid.

5. Take two baking trays and line each with greaseproof paper. Fill a piping bag fitted with the nozzle with the macaron mix. Pipe circles onto the greaseproof paper (you can use a pre-made template if you are worried about the size – I usually count a few seconds in my head to make sure I use the same amount of batter for each shell). Leave the shells to dry for about 20 minutes.

6. Preheat the oven to 165°C fan (365°F/gas 5).

7. Bake the shells for about 13 minutes, turning the tray halfway through for an even bake. Once baked, leave to cool, then the shells will easily come off the greaseproof paper.

8. Make the ganache: in a pan, heat the cream to the point of boiling. Place the chocolate squares in a heatproof bowl and pour the hot cream on top. Mix well with a spatula until the ganache is smooth, then transfer to the fridge for 15 minutes for the ganache to harden.

9. Assemble the macarons: fill a piping bag fitted with the nozzle with the ganache. Find shells that match in terms of size, then pipe one shell with some ganache and place the second shell on top. Transfer to the fridge for at least one day (or overnight) before eating. This is so important because your macarons need to take on the moisture of the fridge to be delicious!

TRUFFES AU CHOCOLAT

Chocolate Truffles

I remember making these with my sister at Mamie Gilberte's just before Christmas. Our hands and mouths were covered in chocolate, and that is why we loved making them so much! They are little chocolate ganache balls, covered with cocoa powder or dessicated coconut, perfect to put on the Christmas table for a midnight snack.

Makes: 12

Ingredients:

200g (7oz) dark chocolate (60–70% cocoa solids)
30g (1oz) salted butter
50ml (2fl oz/3 tbsp) double (heavy) cream
a pinch of sea salt
30g (1oz/¼ cup) icing (confectioners') sugar
2 tbsp Baileys (optional)

FOR THE COATING:
50g (2oz/scant ½ cup) unsweetened cocoa powder
50g (2oz/generous ½ cup) desiccated (dried shredded) coconut
50g (2oz/ scant ½ cup) roasted hazelnuts, finely chopped

1. In a pan, melt the chocolate, butter, cream, sea salt and icing sugar over a low heat, stirring with a spatula. (Alternatively, you can do this in the microwave on medium power). If using the Baileys, add it now.

2. Transfer the mixture to a bowl, cover and leave to harden in the fridge for at least 2 hours. It should be hard like a ganache.

3. Use a spoon to scoop out 1 teaspoon of the mixture, and form into balls of chocolate with your hands. Place the cocoa powder, coconut and roasted hazelnuts in bowls and roll the balls in them to coat.

4. These will keep in a container in the fridge for a couple of weeks.

PALETS BRETONS

Breton Shortbread

Our regional shortbread, true *palets Bretons* have a taste of salted butter.

Makes: 12

Special equipment: a standard baking tray

Ingredients:

2 egg yolks
100g (3½oz/scant ½ cup) caster (superfine) sugar
100g (3½oz) salted butter, at room temperature
1 tsp vanilla bean paste or vanilla extract
140g (5oz/generous 1 cup) plain (all-purpose) flour
½ tsp baking powder

1. In a bowl, whisk the egg yolks with the sugar for a couple of minutes until it becomes white and moussey. Whisk in the butter and vanilla, then stir in the flour and baking powder.

2. Roll the dough into a sausage shape about 5cm (2in) thick and 12cm (5in) long. Wrap in cling film (plastic wrap) and put in the fridge for 3 hours.

3. Preheat the oven to 150°C fan (325°F/gas 3) and line a baking tray with baking paper.

4. Cut 1cm (½in) thick slices from the rolls and lay them flat on the tray, evenly spaced. Bake for 15–18 minutes until golden on the outside. Leave to cool completely before serving.

5. These will keep for 2 weeks in an airtight container.

NOUGAT

Nougat

Nougat reminds me of going to the fair with my parents. The recipe might sound intimidating, but it is actually quite a straightforward process, and it works like magic! It is another satisfying recipe you can make at home and then proudly gift to your friends or eat with a coffee in the afternoon. You can make this with the help of a thermometer or by just trying your luck.

Makes: 15 pieces

Special equipment:

a standard baking tray, sugar thermometer

Ingredients:

50g (2oz/⅓ cup) pistachio nuts
50g (2oz/⅓ cup) hazelnuts
100g (3½oz/⅔ cup) whole almonds
20g (¾oz/4 tsp) vegetable oil
175g (6oz/1½ cups) clear honey
300g (10oz/1⅓ cups) caster (superfine) sugar
2 tbsp water
1 egg white
a pinch of salt
2 tbsp of cornflour, for dusting

1. Preheat the oven to 180°C fan (400°F/gas 6).

2. Scatter the nuts over a baking tray and roast them in the oven for 10–15 minutes until golden. Set aside.

3. Line a baking tray with baking paper and brush it with some oil. Prepare another oiled baking paper sheet to place on top of the nougat to flatten it.

4. In a pan, heat the honey, sugar and water over a high heat and bring to the boil, then cook for 3–5 minutes until it starts to thicken (dip a spoon in and it should drip like a thick syrup) or it reaches 143°C (289°F) on the sugar thermometer.

5. In the meantime, start to whisk the egg white with a pinch of salt until it reaches soft peaks. It should be done at the same time as the syrup, then gently add the syrup while whisking on medium speed. The mixture will double in size.

6. Quickly stir in the nuts with a spatula, then spread the mixture over the baking tray in an even layer. Place the other oiled baking tray on top and flatten the nougat to 1.5cm (¾in) thick. Leave to cool at room temperature, then leave in the fridge overnight.

7. Dust with the cornflour to avoid stickiness and slice with an oiled knife into little rectangles. Store in an airtight container for up to 2 weeks.

PETIT BEURRE

Small Butter Biscuits

A classic little French biscuit, *petit beurre* have four corners for the seasons, 52 dents for the 52 weeks in a year, and 24 little holes for the 24 hours in a day. I remember carefully eating the four corners first, then the dents, then finishing with the rest of the buttery biscuit. My daughter Fleur already loves them, just as I did when I was her age.

Makes: 30

Special equipment:

3 baking trays, *petit beurre* cookie cutter (5 x 10cm/2 x 4in)

Ingredients:

100g (3½oz) salted butter, melted
110g (4oz/½ cup) caster (superfine) sugar
65g (2½oz/4 tbsp) water
250g (9oz/2 cups) plain (all-purpose) flour, plus extra for dusting
½ tsp baking powder

1. In a bowl, combine the melted butter, sugar and water with a spatula to create a paste. Add the flour and baking powder and mix to form a ball. Tip out onto your worktop and knead for a couple of minutes, then cover with cling film (plastic wrap) and leave to rest in the fridge for a couple of hours to firm up.

2. Preheat the oven to 180°C fan (400°F/gas 6).

3. Flour your worktop and roll the dough into a large rectangle of 2–3mm ($\frac{1}{16}$in) thickness. Cut out the biscuits using a cookie cutter and place on baking trays lined with baking paper or silicon mats. You can fit about 10 biscuits on each baking tray.

4. Bake for 15 minutes until the edges are golden and the biscuit is paler on the inside. Leave to cool completely, then store in an airtight container for up to 1 week.

Tip: You can write different messages onto your biscuits with icing pens, they make a really cute present for any celebration.

MINI CANELÉS

Mini Canelés

This recipe comes from my uncle's grandma, directly from Bordeaux, where they are from. Winemakers used to use egg whites to clarify the wine in the barrels, leaving a lot of spare egg yolks to use up! It is a very simple batter, flavoured with vanilla and rum, which caramelises during baking but still stays very soft and chewy inside.

Makes: 30–40 mini canelés or 12 large canelés

Special equipment:

silicon mini canelés mould or 12 normal size canelé moulds

Ingredients:

500ml (18fl oz/2 cups) whole milk
1 tsp vanilla bean paste or extract
2 eggs, plus 2 egg yolks
250g (9oz/2 cups) icing (confectioners') sugar
3 tbsp rum
110g (4oz/scant 1 cup) plain (all-purpose) flour
50g (2oz) salted butter, melted, plus extra for greasing

1. Bring the milk to the boil in a pan over a high heat, remove and leave to cool. Once cool, add the vanilla.

2. In a large bowl, mix the eggs and egg yolks with the icing sugar, then add the rum, 1 tablespoon at a time. Stir in the flour and mix, before adding the melted butter and then the milk. Cover and transfer to the fridge to rest overnight.

3. Preheat the oven to 220°C fan (475°F/gas 9), grease the moulds and place a baking tray inside the oven to heat.

4. Fill the moulds to three-quarters full, place on a baking tray and bake for 30 minutes. Reduce the oven to 200°C fan (425°F/gas 7). Bake for 15 minutes, then reduce the oven to 180°C fan (400°F/gas 6) and bake for a final 45 minutes. (If using large moulds, bake for 20 minutes at 220°C/475°F/gas 9 and 1 hour at 180°C fan/400°F/gas 6.)

MACARONS À LA NOIX DE COCO

Coconut Macaroons

Another coconut recipe! If you know a little bit about French history and geography, you might know that French cuisine has a Caribbean influence due to the overseas territories of France, *les DOM-TOM*, especially islands like Réunion, Guadeloupe or Martinique. These cute little macaroons are easy to make and they are always a great treat to have with coffee or tea with friends.

Makes: 20

Special equipment: a standard baking tray

Ingredients:

100g (3½oz/scant ½ cup) caster (superfine) sugar
200g (7oz/2¼ cups) desiccated (dried shredded) coconut
2 large egg whites (60g/2oz)

EXTRA:
100g (3½oz) dark chocolate (70% cocoa solids)

1. Preheat the oven to 200°C fan (425°F/gas 7).

2. In a very clean bowl, combine the sugar and the desiccated coconut, then whisk in the egg whites – it should be a chunky paste.

3. Line a baking tray with baking paper or a silicon mat, then drop 1 teaspoon of the mixture at a time on the paper to make some little rock-like cookies.

4. Bake for 10 minutes; they will start to brown on the outside but you want them to stay chewy on the inside.

5. Leave to cool completely before eating.

Tip: You can melt some chocolate and dip the bottom of the cookies into it to make them even more delicious!

COOKIES TROIS FAÇONS

Cookies Three Ways

The way you like your cookies is very personal. Crunchy, soft, warm, cold, with chocolate, without chocolate, gooey, cakey – lots of options! These cookies are in between crunchy and soft – I like to undercook them to get some gooeyness inside. Here are three different cookies, to suit a variety of tastes. The quantities given for each different version will be enough for a third of a batch of cookies; if you want to stick to just one flavour, triple the quantities given.

Makes: 18 large cookies

Special equipment:

large baking tray, ice cream scoop (optional)

Ingredients:

220g (8oz) salted butter, melted
150g (5oz/generous ¾ cup) light brown sugar
200g (7oz/scant 1 cup) granulated sugar
2 large eggs
330g (11½oz/2⅔ cups) plain (all-purpose) flour
1 tsp baking powder
1 tsp bicarbonate of soda (baking soda)
½ tsp salt

FOR A CHOCOLATE AND NUT VERSION:
100g (3½oz/1 cup) nuts (hazelnuts, walnuts, almonds)
200g (7oz/generous 1 cup) milk chocolate chips

FOR A BLUEBERRY AND CHOCOLATE VERSION:
50g (2oz/scant ½ cup) dried blueberries
200g (7oz/scant 1 cup) white chocolate chips

FOR A SEA SALT AND DARK CHOCOLATE VERSION:
200g (7oz/generous 1 cup) dark chocolate chunks
a couple of pinches of sea salt, to serve

1. Preheat the oven to 180°C fan (400°F/gas 6).

2. Melt the butter with the sugars in a pan over a medium heat, stirring with a wooden spatula. Transfer to a mixing bowl and stir in the eggs.

3. Combine the flour, baking powder, bicarbonate of soda and salt, and add this to the mixing bowl and stir in. Once you have a uniform batter, you can divide it among 3 small bowls and add the flavourings to each, or you can just stick to one flavouring.

4. Divide the batter into even-sized balls (for large cookies: 60g/2oz; for small cookies: 30g/1oz) using an ice cream scoop or your hands and place in the fridge for at least 1 hour to firm up.

5. Place 5 small cookies (or 3 big ones) onto your baking tray, evenly spaced apart to allow for spread, and cook for 12–14 minutes. Sprinkle some sea salt on the dark chocolate cookies.

Tip: This recipe makes a lot of cookies, but I always freeze half of my raw batch, freezing the little balls in pairs or individually.

MINI FONDANTS AU CHOCOLAT

Mini Chocolate Fondants

My cousin Alexandre and I shared a flat at uni in Rennes. His papa, *Tonton* Jean Charles, not only made him delicious homemade food from the restaurant they have been running for 30 years, Le Bretagne in Fougères, but he also froze some chocolate fondant for us ... total dream student life! Here is my version of these treats, which you can serve immediately or you can part-bake, leave to cool and freeze for a midnight snack or last-minute dessert.

Serves: 6

Special equipment:

silicon muffin moulds or ramekins (if not unmoulding)

Ingredients:

150g (5oz) salted butter, at room temperature, plus 1 tbsp for greasing
150g (5oz/1¼ cups) icing (confectioners') sugar
3 large eggs
50g (2oz/scant ½ cup) plain (all-purpose) flour
200g (7oz) chocolate (70–80% cocoa solids)

1. Cream the butter and icing sugar together in a bowl with a whisk, then alternate adding the eggs, one by one, with the flour, spoonful by spoonful, stirring to incorporate.

2. Melt the chocolate using a bain marie or in a bowl in the microwave (see p. 13), then pour into the batter.

3. Grease the silicon muffin moulds or ramekins with butter, then fill them three-quarters full with the batter. Put the moulds in the freezer for 1 hour.

4. Preheat the oven to 150°C fan (325°F/gas 3) and cook the fondants from frozen for 20–25 minutes. Once cooked, wait 10 minutes for them to cool down before removing them from their moulds, and serve with *Crème Anglaise* or *Crème Chantilly* (see p. 171).

GUIMAUVES ENROBÉES DE CHOCOLAT

Chocolate-covered Marshmallows

The only thing I asked my parents to bring over for me when I first moved to London were *ourson au chocolat*, which are little marshmallow bears covered with chocolate. To this day, they might be my number one sweet. The recipe here is a simple way for you to make your own marshmallow – which is very satisfying, I have to say – then you can dip them into a bowl of chocolate to coat.

Makes: 30 marshmallow squares

Special equipment: rectangular baking tray, skewers

Ingredients:

6 sheets of gelatine (20g/¾oz)
1 tbsp oil, for greasing
50g (2oz/scant ½ cup) cornflour (cornstarch), plus extra for dusting
50g (2oz/scant ½ cup) icing (confectioners') sugar, plus extra for dusting
100g (3½oz) egg whites (3 large eggs)
a pinch of salt
200g (7oz/scant 1 cup) caster (superfine) sugar
3 tbsp water
1 tsp vanilla extract
200g (7oz) dark or milk chocolate

1. Place the gelatine sheets in a bowl of cold water to soften while you make the meringue. Oil a baking tray and line it with baking paper – the oil will help it stay in place.

2. Combine the cornflour and icing sugar in a bowl, then sprinkle a couple of tablespoons over the baking paper.

3. Whisk the egg whites with a pinch of salt in the bowl of an electric mixer on medium speed.

4. Meanwhile, heat the sugar and water in a pan over a medium heat to dissolve the sugar. Increase the heat for a couple of minutes until you get a sugar syrup. Drain the gelatine and squeeze out any excess water, then add it to the sugar syrup, stirring with a spatula.

5. By now, the egg whites should have tripled in size and become thick and glossy. Add the vanilla extract, then slowly pour in the sugar syrup, while still mixing, to make the marshmallow. Rapidly spread the marshmallow onto the prepared baking tray and make it as flat as possible using the spatula. Sprinkle with some extra cornflour and icing sugar mix and leave to set for at least an hour at room temperature.

6. Turn the marshmallow upside down onto a dusted worktop and remove the baking paper (keep it for later). Slice the marshmallow into little squares and sprinkle generously with the rest of the icing sugar and cornflour mix.

7. Melt the chocolate in a bain marie or in a bowl in the microwave. Secure one square of marshmallow with a skewer and dip either all or just the bottom of the marshmallow into the melted chocolate. Place back onto the baking paper on the tray and leave to set (you can place it in the fridge for an hour to speed up the process).

8. Store in an airtight container for up to 2 weeks.

PETITS EXTRAS

Accompaniments

Serving your cake or dessert with the 'little extras' featured in this chapter is bound to make everyone at the table even more appreciative! Throughout the book, I have given you some ideas of what to serve dishes with, but you can always experiment and mix and match. There are some decadent additions (Kinder Bueno Sauce, p. 174) or some simpler options (Chantilly Cream, p. 171). I have also added a couple of simple jam recipes to show you how easy it is to make (p. 176–7), as my family are avid jam makers!

CRÈME ANGLAISE

Vanilla Pouring Custard

Although the literal translation means 'English cream', this is not the same as English custard. More liquid and lighter in texture, it is the perfect addition to my *Gâteau Simple au Chocolat* (Easy Moist Chocolate Cake, p. 68) or to pour on top of the *Tarte Bourdaloue Tonka* (Almond, Pear and Tonka Bean Tart, p. 102).

Serves: 6–8

Ingredients:

500ml (18fl oz/2 cups) whole milk
5 egg yolks
100g (3½oz/scant ½ cup) caster (superfine) sugar
1 vanilla pod or 1 tbsp vanilla bean paste

1. Bring the milk to the boil in a pan over a high heat. In the meantime, whisk the egg yolks with the sugar until airy and lighter in colour.

2. When the milk is just boiling, pour over the egg yolks and whisk vigorously. Pour the cream back into the pan and gently cook over a low heat, constantly stirring with a spatula. The *crème anglaise* is done when a thick layer coats the spatula.

3. Serve warm.

CRÈME CHANTILLY

Chantilly Cream

Probably the most-used *petits extras* recipe in my home. When friends catch me off guard and arrive for *le goûter* or a last-minute dinner, I make an even simpler version, by just mixing crème fraîche, a teaspoon of icing sugar and a tablespoon of vanilla bean paste.

Serves: 6–8 servings

Ingredients:

300ml (10fl oz/1¼ cups) very cold double (heavy) cream
25g (1oz/scant ¼ cup) icing (confectioners') sugar
1 tsp vanilla extract or vanilla bean paste

1. Place the cream in the freezer for 5–10 minutes if it isn't cold enough. Pour it into the bowl of an electric mixer fitted with the whisk attachment along with the icing sugar and the vanilla, and start to whisk on medium speed for a few minutes. Be careful not to over-whisk it – if you dip a spatula in, it should create a soft peak.

2. Store in the fridge for up to 3 days in an airtight container.

COULIS À LA FRAMBOISE

Raspberry Sauce

Dolloped on top of *Gaufres* (Waffles, p. 135) or with the *Gâteau aux Pommes et Calvados de Mamie* (Mamie's Calvados Apple Cake, p. 49), this coulis will add some tart and zingy sweetness to your bake!

Makes: 6–8 servings

Ingredients:

500g (1lb 2oz) fresh raspberries (or frozen, but defrosted)
100g (3½oz/scant ½ cup) caster (superfine) sugar
2 tbsp water

1. In a pan over a low heat, heat the raspberries, sugar and water and bring to the boil, stirring with a spatula all the time, to break up the raspberries. You can push the coulis through a metal sieve to remove the pips if you would like a silky smooth coulis, or just serve pips and all.

2. Serve warm or cold. Keeps for 2 weeks in a sealed jar in the fridge.

COULIS AU CHOCOLAT

Chocolate Sauce

Perfect for pouring over ice cream, crêpes, cakes, waffles, profiteroles, fruits, etc. ... anything you want to add a little bit of chocolate to.

Makes: 6 servings/1 cup

Ingredients:

100g (3½oz) dark chocolate (60–80% cocoa solids)
20g (¾oz) salted butter
100ml (3½fl oz/scant ½ cup) whole milk
30g (1oz/2 tbsp) caster (superfine) sugar (optional)
1 tbsp crème fraîche

1. In a pan, melt the chocolate with the butter over a medium heat for a couple of minutes. Add the milk, the sugar (if using) and the crème fraîche and use a spatula to mix it together.

2. Serve hot.

Tip: If not using immediately, reheat it in the microwave for 30 seconds.

GLACE VANILLE

Vanilla Ice Cream

I am personally quite particular about ice cream, and it has to be a 'good one' for me to want to indulge. This is a 'good one'!

Makes: 6–8 servings

Ingredients:

360ml (12fl oz/scant 1½ cups) sweetened condensed milk
a pinch of salt
1 tbsp vanilla bean paste
600ml (20fl oz/2½ cups) very cold double (heavy) cream

1. Put the condensed milk, salt and vanilla bean paste into a large bowl. Set aside.
2. In a separate bowl, whip the cold cream with an electric mixer for 3–5 minutes until it triples in size.
3. Add the cream to the condensed milk and use a spatula to create a soft custard.
4. Pour into a freezerproof container with a lid, seal and freeze for at least 2 hours.

SAUCE FAÇON BUENO

Kinder Bueno Sauce

My obsession with Kinder continues! This is an accurate version of the cream inside the Kinder Bueno. It couldn't be more perfect with Crêpes (Pancakes, p. 124) or served with the *Mini Fondants au Chocolat* (Mini Chocolate Fondants, p. 162). A fun game is to make your guests guess what it is!

Makes: 1 jar/2 cups

Ingredients:

250g (9oz/scant 2 cups) hazelnuts
200g (7oz) white chocolate

1. Preheat the oven to 180°C fan (400°F/gas 6).
2. Place the hazelnuts on a baking tray and roast them for 10–12 minutes until they are golden.
3. Use a food processor to blitz the nuts to make a hazelnut butter. It will take 3–5 minutes for the oils to release and create a smooth butter texture.
4. Melt the white chocolate in a bowl in the microwave, then add the hazelnut butter and stir the two together to combine. Pour into an airtight container. This will keep for up to a month in the fridge.

SAUCE CARAMEL AU BEURRE SALÉ

Caramel and Salted Butter Sauce

A classic Breton sauce which is a great way to learn how to make caramel. I love it on top of some *Pommes au Four* (Baked Apples, p. 26) or for dessert with some *Glace Vanille* (Vanilla Ice Cream, p. 173).

Makes: 6–8 servings

Ingredients:

250g (9oz/generous 1 cup) caster (superfine) sugar
60ml (2fl oz/¼ cup) water
130ml (4½fl oz/generous ½ cup) double (heavy) cream
60g (2oz) salted butter
½ tsp sea salt

1. In a pan, bring the sugar and water to the boil. Leave to cook until it becomes a lovely caramel colour, around 4–6 minutes.

2. Remove from the heat and gently add the cream using a spatula to stir (it will bubble and steam). Put back on the heat and bring it back to the boil.

3. Remove from the heat, then add the butter and the sea salt, and mix well for a uniform caramel.

4. Pour into a container with a lid. This can be kept for up to a month in the fridge.

SAUCE AUX SPECULOOS

Speculoos Sauce

From our cousins the Belgians, *speculoos* (or Lotus biscuits) are sweet, crumbly, cinnamon biscuits that are often served with a coffee at bars and restaurants. I discovered this sauce in Bruges, then I was hooked!

Makes: 1 jar/2 cups

Ingredients:

200g (7oz) speculoos (Lotus biscuits)
40g (1½oz/¼ cup) brown sugar
100ml (3½fl oz/scant ½ cup) whole milk
50g (2oz) salted butter

1. Use a food processor to whiz the speculoos and the brown sugar to a powder.

2. In a pan, heat the milk and the butter together, and when the butter has melted add to the food processor. Mix for a few seconds to create a smooth paste.

3. Pour into an airtight container and leave to cool completely for it to thicken. This will keep for up to a month in the fridge.

CONFITURE DE FRAISES DE MAMAN

Maman's Strawberry Jam

Maman and my mamies make kilos of jams every year. They either buy strawberries from the local grocer or harvest their own fruits at home. I remember it being a summer thing, when my papa would bring 10kg of rhubarb for me and my sister to peel and slice and for Maman to soak overnight.

Makes: 2 jars

Ingredients:

800g (1¾lb) fresh strawberries, roughly chopped
400g (14oz/1¾ cups) caster (superfine) sugar
juice of 1 lemon
1 tbsp salted butter

1. Put the chopped strawberries into a pan with the sugar and the lemon juice. Bring to the boil, then simmer for 20–30 minutes. Some white foam might form on top, but don't worry, add the butter and gently stir to release it. Leave to cool.

2. Fill two clean, sterilised jars (see tip) with the jam and seal tightly. This will keep at room temperature in the sealed jar for a few months.

Tip: You can sterilise the jars by washing them in hot soapy water and putting them in the oven set to a low heat for 20 minutes.

CONFITURE DE RHUBARBE ET PRUNEAUX DE MAMIE

Mamie's Rhubarb and Prune Jam

When I asked Mamie Suzanne for this recipe, her eyes lit up. This is one of my Papa's favourite jams, and it has been made for decades. As children, we fought to eat the prunes first. Their sweetness balances the tartness of the rhubarb, a match made in heaven!

Makes: 2 jars/4 cups

Ingredients:

800g (1¾lb) fresh rhubarb
400g (14oz/1¾ cups) caster (superfine) sugar
10 prunes, pitted and cut in half

1. Wash and dice the rhubarb – you don't have to peel it, but some of the strings will come off while chopping it. Put the chunks in a large bowl and sprinkle the sugar on top. Cover and leave for a couple of hours, or ideally overnight, to release the juices.

2. Put the rhubarb and juices in a pan and bring to the boil, then simmer for 30–45 minutes. Add the prunes after 15 minutes.

3. When the rhubarb is still piping hot, fill two clean, sterilised jars (see tip above) with the jam and seal tightly. The jam will keep at room temperature for a few months.

CONFITURE DE FIGUES

Fig Jam

If my parents go down to see my uncle and auntie in September for fig season, you know they will come back with kilos of figs to make jams. It couldn't be easier to make and is delicious not only with cakes but also with pâté, cheese or even meat.

Serves: 2 jars/4 cups

Ingredients:

800g (1¾lb) fresh figs
400g (14oz/1¾ cups) caster (superfine) sugar
juice of 1 lemon

1. Wash and quarter the figs, then add to the pan with the sugar and the lemon juice. Bring to the boil and simmer for 20–30 minutes.

2. Fill two clean, sterilised jars with the jam (see tip opposite) and seal tightly. The jam will keep at room temperature for a few months.

GLAÇAGE AU MASCARPONE

Mascarpone Icing

Although not very French, this is my go-to icing. It is ideal for elevating a *Gâteau au Yaourt* (Yoghurt Cake, p. 53), or to sweeten the *Gâteau Aux Abricots, Amande Et Lavande* (Apricot, Almond and Lavender Cake p. 60).

Makes: enough to ice 1 cake/2 cups

Ingredients

240g (9oz/generous 1 cup) mascarpone cheese
1 tsp vanilla extract
100g (3½oz/generous ¾ cup) icing (confectioners') sugar
240ml (9fl oz/1 cup) double (heavy) cream
a pinch of salt

1. In the bowl of an electric mixer fitted with the paddle attachment, beat the mascarpone on medium speed for 30 seconds. Still mixing, add the vanilla and gradually add the icing sugar. Do not overmix as you don't want it to curdle.

2. Mixing on high speed, pour in the double cream and salt and whisk for 1–3 minutes until light and fluffy.

GANACHE AU CHOCOLAT ET GANACHE MONTÉE

Chocolate Ganache or Whipped Ganache

A French classic, this thick and glossy ganache can be served warm to complement ice cream or to serve with the Crème Brulée (p. 38). I also use it whipped (*ganache montée*) to ice my *Gâteau Simple au Chocolat* (Easy Moist Chocolate Cake, p. 68), which makes the best chocolate cake ever!

Makes: enough to ice 1 cake/2 cups

Ingredients:

250g (9oz) dark chocolate (50% cocoa solids)
200ml (7fl oz/scant 1 cup) double (heavy) cream
50g (2oz) salted butter

1. Melt the chocolate in a bain marie or in a bowl in the microwave. Bring the double cream almost to the boil in a pan.

2. Pour half of the hot cream on top of the chocolate and use a spatula to stir energetically. Add the rest of the cream and stir thoroughly to achieve a uniform ganache.

3. Finish the ganache with the butter and stir until it is completely melted and incorporated. Place in the fridge for at least 1 hour until it sets.

4. If you want to make a *ganache montée*, simply pour the ganache into the bowl of an electric mixer and whisk for a couple of minutes. You will get an airy and lighter-coloured ganache, the perfect consistency to ice a tiered cake.

GANACHE AU CHOCOLAT BLANC

White Chocolate Ganache or Whipped Ganache

Just like the dark chocolate version, this a sweeter and milder version of a ganache. You can spread it on some *Petit Pains au Lait* (Milk Bread, p. 132) use it to complement your *Financiers au Beurre Noisette* (Brown Butter Financiers, p. 143).

Makes: enough to ice 1 cake/2 cups

Ingredients:

400g (14oz) white chocolate
140ml (5fl oz/scant ⅔ cup) double (heavy) cream

1. Melt the white chocolate carefully in a bain marie or in a bowl in the microwave. Bring the double cream just to the boil in a pan.

2. Pour half of the cream on top of the chocolate and use a spatula to stir energetically. Add the rest of the cream and stir well in order to achieve a uniform ganache. Place in the fridge for at least 1 hour until it sets.

Tip: For a whipped white chocolate ganache, follow the instructions in Step 4 opposite.

INDEX

E

F

G

H

I

Merci

I would first like to thank my number-one fan and cake critic, my husband Luke, for never saying no to a piece of cake, and for supporting me throughout the process of writing my book. Then my number-two fan, Joey Swarbrick, my manager and agent since the beginning of my career, for always believing in me. Thank you to Kate Pollard, my publisher, for trusting me to write the book and for guiding me through the process, and to everyone at Welbeck Publishing for giving me the opportunity to create and write my first cookbook. Thank you also to my literary agent, Antony Topping, who helped me to turn my initial book idea into a reality.

Thanks go to the incredible team of people who helped to create the book: Nassima Rothacker, for your amazing photography and lovely self; Frankie Unsworth, for understanding my vision from day one with the props and food styling; Vanessa Masci, for designing the most beautiful book and really making it 'me'; and to everyone who helped on the shoots: cake extraordinaire Julia Aden, editor Matt Tomlinson, as well as photography assistants Amy Grover and Sam Reeves, and props assistant Georgia Rudd.

I'd also like to thank Caroline Moyes Matheou, who at the last minute cast a discerning eye over my text, proofreading it concisely and with a caring touch. And Margaux Durigon, who checked my French at the eleventh hour. Thank you to my girl gang, who I have been talking to about the book over the last two years – you have been the best of friends and have given me so much love and support.

And finally, thank you to my family, the Lagrèves and the Coquelins, for the most fun and loving childhood and teenage years, fuelled by the best food and wine!

About the Author

Raised in a small village in Brittany, Manon Lagrève grew up on a farm where food was celebrated as the core of family life. She learned to cook from watching her mother and grandmothers make every meal from scratch – from breads to biscuits, and, of course, desserts.

At the age of 20, she traded rural France for the lure of the big city – Manon moved to London to work as an au pair with the hope of becoming fluent in English. In 2018, Manon entered *The Great British Bake Off* (*The Great British Baking Show*), where she won Star Baker in the first week for her biscuits and reached the quarter final. In 2023 she appeared once again on the *The Great British Bake Off* New Year special, competing against previous finalists, and won the episode.

For the past four years, she has been sharing her baking creations and food inspirations online, gaining a loyal community on Instagram and TikTok. Her 'Tuesday Bake Along' videos have encouraged thousands to try their hand at baking. Her recipes and bakes are inspired by her French heritage, modern London and the many places she continues to visit and explore around the world.

Manon has worked with KitchenAid, Tefal, the French Ministry of Agriculture, and has been ambassador for several French brands, including LeCreuset, Citroën and l'Occitane. Manon also runs her own fashion and lifestyle brand, Manon and Rose, that she mostly wears throughout the book.

Manon lives in London with her English husband, Luke, and their daughter, Fleur.

@manonlagreve @manonandrose

www.manonlagreve.com

Published in 2023 by OH Editions,
part of Welbeck Publishing Group.
Offices in: London – 20 Mortimer Street, London W1T 3JW
& Sydney – 205 Commonwealth Street, Surry Hills 2010
www.welbeckpublishing.com

A CIP catalogue record for this book is available from the British Library.

UK ISBN 978-1-80453-015-3
US ISBN 978-1-80453-055-9

Publisher: Kate Pollard
In-house editor: Matt Tomlinson
Editors: Helena Caldon and Emily Preece-Morrison
Design and illustrations: Vanessa Masci
Prop and food stylist: Frankie Unsworth
Indexer: Cathy Heath
Production controller: Arlene Alexander
Colour reproduction: p2d

Printed and bound by Leo in China

MIX
Paper | Supporting responsible forestry
FSC® C020056

10 9 8 7 6 5 4 3